South Pennine Escort
– *from Edale to Ilkley Moor*

Michael Z. Brooke

Sigma Press ● Wilmsow

First published in 1987 by

Sigma Press 98a Water Lane, Wilmslow, SK9 5BB, England.

Typeset by **Minstrel Publications Limited,** Sale, M33 2BY, England.

Printed in Malta by Interprint Limited

ISBN 1 85058 069 3

British Library Cataloguing in Publication Data

Brooke, Michael Z.
    South Pennine Escort – from Edale to Ilkley Moor
    1. Pennine Chain (England) – Description and travel
    I. Title
    914.281   DA670.P4

Cover Photograph: the beauty of the area is captured in this photograph *Walking on Howarth Moor* by Simon Warner – a talented local professional photographer.

Foreword

The South Pennines is a unique and fascinating area at the centre of Britain, the village green of Northern England.

It is an area of dramatic views, from the wild, wide, open moorland plateau to the deeply incised river valleys; roaring tumbling streams and sheltered woodland glades; hillside hamlets amidst their webs of drystone walls contrasting with tight valley towns clustered round sturdy Pennine mills and proud non-conformist chapels.

The whole history of human endeavour is on display. Early man, destroyer of the upland forests settled on the hilltops. Stone axes made little impression on the lowland vale and insect ridden moist valleys harboured disease. Celtic camps and Roman roads indicate later colonization.

Exposure to the weather destroyed the upland soils. Farming gravitated to the shoulders of the hills where waves of invaders – Danes, Norsemen and Anglo-Saxons have left their mark in local placenames and local dialects.

Life was hard and gregarious too. Any income supplement was welcome. Local sheep, hardy enough to survive life on the open plateau provided the answer. Local wool, ingenuity and thrift. Family enterprise. All employed, from the youngest to the oldest, in the production of cloth. Children combed, spinsters spun and men wove. The skill and enterprise of the Pennine people laid the foundations for the Industrial Revolution – making, selling, marketing and distributing cloth all over Britain and Europe, even Russia and the Middle East – all leaving the hills on horseback. The first truly industrial society in the world, totally dependent upon manufacturing industry.

Pennine merchants grew rich and built stone houses, fine Elizabethan and Jacobean mansions. When technology found ways to harness water power their capital built the mills, first in the narrow tributary valleys, then in the major Trans-Pennine valleys with the move to steam power. Pack-horse tracks gave way to turnpikes, canals and eventually railways – but still the Pennines were at the centre of this new way of life. Todmorden once held the largest factory in the world.

But not for long. Initiative began to ebb away and people of initiative followed. The action shifted to the edges of the hills and then even further afield. Wonderful soft Pennine water no longer attracted industry here. It was instead collected and piped further afield.

Pennine towns declined, some to less than half their former population. Forgotten and forlorn. A veneer of dirt, disorder and dereliction spread across the area.

But Pennine people are not easily defeated. Redefinition of local resources has reversed a century of decline. Once wool and water power, today's resources are that unique blend of spectacular scenery, history and industrial heritage.

Rediscovery is on the agenda. People travel thousands of miles to look at stones – stones in the desert, by the oceans, wherever man has settled – milestones in the evolution of human culture, pyramids, temples, cathedrals. Here in the South Pennines are the milestones of the greatest leap forward mankind has ever seen – the industrial revolution. The whole transition from an agrarian to an industrial way of life is on show, from the domestic workshops and early cloth halls of the 15th and 16th centuries to the present.

Imagine the packhorse trains jogging from Heptonstall to Hebden Bridge to cross the old bridge. When walking part of our rich footpath network, spare a thought for the early workers who cut these paths, commuting to work on clogs from their hillside homes to the factory by the stream far below.

Visit Hebden Bridge, the Pennine Centre, natural focus for the area and wonder at its steep terraces of workers' houses, stacked high up the hillsides, built one on top of the other, double-decker houses, top and bottom houses, quickly constructed to accommodate the rush into the factory era.

No longer a forgotten area, the South Pennines is now beginning to get the care and protection it deserves. Local people and local enterprise have again seized the opportunity to use local resources for a new future.

Facilities have been created and information provided. Come, visit, enjoy and respect our area. Discover for yourself this great story of human endeavour in its superb scenic setting!

DAVID E FLETCHER
Chairman, Pennine Heritage

Pennine Heritage is an independent voluntary organization registered as a company limited by guarantee and a charitable trust. It seeks to assist the social, economic and environmental recovery of the area in partnership with others. It has an ambitious programme of activity and welcomes your assistance. Further information may be obtained from the Birchcliffe Centre, Hebden Bridge or through reading Pennine Magazine, obtainable at most newsagents.

CONTENTS

Acknowledgements

Numbers of people have helped to write this book – many unknowingly, most anonymously. All have shown the good-humoured friendliness for which the South Pennines are famous.

Much of the information has come from casual encounters in pubs, restaurants, libraries, information centres and along the highways and byways of the region. Especial thanks go to: Ron Buckley (who drew the pictures), David Fletcher (who wrote the foreword), Alan Gaskell (who read the whole book and checked the routes), and Michael Hurford, Anne Hynes, Eileen Smith, Sylvia Tavares-Mellor, Shirley Wise and Averil Wood (who gave advice and assistance).

Finally I must thank my wife, Hilda, and my family who accompanied me on many visits to the area and helped in numerous ways, and my secretary, Elizabeth Hickson who typed the manuscript and drew the charts.

How to use this book

South Pennine Escort is designed to be your trusty guide to this fascinating and unusual region.

The seven routes cater for a variety of interests. The first two (Edale and Glossop) take you into some of the wildest country. Stalybridge and Saddleworth, route 3, offers history and nature, as does Littleborough route 4 – the least known area described in the book. Route 5 centres round Hebden Bridge, route 6 starts in the land of the Brontës, and finally Ilkley Moor is known almost everywhere but less often visited.

Each route:

introduces the area;
tells you how to get there;
lists some local sports and hobbies;
suggests places for food, accommodation and shopping;
proposes some walking routes (with likely timings), and some driving routes in miles;
advises about getting to the next route;
mentions some booklets for further reading.

All the routes have information on sights you may expect to see, including local and natural history. Many of the routes mention items of interest to foreign visitors; there are also hints about taking pushchairs or dogs.

If you have something special in mind, look up the index which lists most of the interests in the book and can guide you to the route that will suit you best.

Introduction

The South Pennines, from Edale to Ilkley Moor

The South Pennines are for real. They provide their sort of pleasure; more gritty and less bland than more conventional beauty spots, tailor made for those who seek a subtle blend of landscape, heritage and entertainment, or are tired of the tourist traps.

The British have to be persuaded that the 'backbone of England' really exists outside the geography lessons of their schooldays. If you are not British, you may not have heard of these hills, but there is a good chance that your fellow countrymen have trodden the Pennines as warriors, merchants, refugees or immigrants.

Whoever you may be, the Pennines offer relaxation with a difference. They lack the beaches or the glaciers of more popular resorts; they also lack the crowds. The hills have coats of many colours, an endless variety of the efforts of nature mixed up with some curious works of man. You can wander in a few miles from a bridge built 4,000 years ago to a hi-tech telescope.

Wild, remote patches, untouched by human hand, are interspersed with the relics of pioneer industries. Ancient remains glare at the concrete megaliths of more modern enterprises. You can be out-of-sight of house or human and yet within a few miles of a city centre.

This is an area alive with conservation, but the normal meaning of the word is turned upside down. Elsewhere 'conservation' is used for the work of rescuing nature from destruction by humans. Here it means saving the works of man from being swamped by nature. Derelict canals, mills, railways, homes are being salvaged from the advancing shrub.

The hills are not high by Everest standards. They go up to about 2,000 feet (a little over 600 metres), but they are always changing, restlessly, unexpectedly; and the changes, so out-of-keeping with their grave appearance, provide the first of countless contrasts. There can be light and darkness, bright sunshine and

1

patches of fog, in quick succession; you can be skiing on the higher slopes while it is raining among the foothills. Oases of quietness and solitude exist between centres of noise and activity.

The Pennines play tricks with their changes, the weather and the terrain can be treacherous. Even the name started as a hoax, when someone forged a Roman diary 250 years ago. He called them the Penine hills, and the name stuck even after the forgery was exposed. The Victorians thought Penine indecent and added the second n.

Men have tramped these hills, among the oldest in the world, since these parts became habitable at all, earning a hard living as the glaciers melted. The most famous invaders – the Romans – had the same idea as the motorway builders of today: find some unspoiled country and run a road across it. No doubt the M62 will soon be buried like the Roman roads, the Pennines have a way of asserting themselves and wrecking the wreckers.

The region is full of footpaths and bridleways; all are uncrowded except the Pennine Way. This famous long-distance path – its official length is about 250 miles – starts at Edale as does this book. We shall follow it in route one and for short distances elsewhere; otherwise we shall leave it alone. It has been described many times, especially by Wainwright who makes all other guides look tame. But do remember that times have changed since he wrote. The path itself is clearer through the tramp of heavy feet; but other landmarks have disappeared, including two of Wainwright's few recommended eating-places in the first forty miles.

We shall go our own way, and give the crowds a miss.

The Routes

This is a book for the inquisitive holidaymaker.

You may come for a day, a weekend, a fortnight, a month, a century if you like. My role is to show you round a few chosen sites – specimens of what the region has to offer. I take it you want to know something of what goes on, but not too much. You do not want to be bored on your holiday, so I have made a selection for you – a little natural history here, a little human history there. Enough to keep you going without giving you indigestion. Of course the expert will say how much has been missed out. Right! So it has. When you have finished with this book, you are on your own. You can switch to DIY and I will be dropping a few hints about how to Do-it-Yourself as well, telling you about the information centres and some of the booklets written by local enthusiasts.

Talking about information centres, these come in many shapes and sizes. On the seven routes, fourteen centres are mentioned, some owned by public authorities and some by voluntary bodies; they do not all exist for the same purposes. Most will provide you with a list of places to stay – but few give more details than just an address, and only one was willing to discuss the quality of accommodation with me. Most call themselves *visitor* centres or *heritage* centres, and these will not usually book accommodation (the *tourist* information centres do that). I found the staff in all of them courteous and helpful, but the depth of knowledge varies. One had apparently not heard of a famous monument a few hundred yards away, and another denied any knowledge of a nature reserve which was, in fact, within an hour's walk; others answered all my out-of-the-way questions without hesitation. At the beginning of each route, I give the phone number of an information centre, but remember that some are only open part-time, especially in winter when opening may be at weekends only. You can obtain more information, including phone numbers, of the places I mention from the information centres.

Selected from many explored, the routes described here are never overcrowded except for brief sections on Sundays. It is taken for granted that you will want to get out of your car, that many readers indeed will prefer to use public transport, and that you will appreciate the opportunities of using your legs when you can. BUT IF YOU CANNOT WALK THERE IS STILL A PLACE FOR YOU IN THIS BOOK.

Each chapter contains suggestions for the carbound – the disabled, the very old and the very young. My aim is to help you to enjoy as much of each route as possible, and to add some views which the walkers do not see to make up for what you miss. Cyclists and horseriders can follow the carbound route, but they may prefer to seek out the quieter bridleways which often bring them to the same destination. Of course you cannot ride on the footpaths, but I have taken my bike over some of the routes described with a mixture of riding, pushing and carrying. On route 6, the carbound follow some roads especially recommended for cyclists.

With the walking routes a time in minutes is given. Naturally this only gives you a rough idea of what you should allow, but it gives a better idea to most of us than distances. I know some readers will criticize my timings – "He says 30 minutes and I did it in 10," I can hear you saying – I've been picturing an average family, not a gang of marathon runners. If you want to work out how long the whole walk might take, remember to add stops for refreshments and just looking around. Unless you know the area well, start looking for somewhere to stay, or for transport back to base, well before sunset.

For the carbound, distances are given and, because you are following a walker's trail, distances are short. You have plenty of time to wander and to look around.

EVEN IF YOU ARE HOUSEBOUND THERE IS STILL A PLACE FOR YOU HERE. Arm yourself with the ordnance survey maps and enjoy the routes from your living room.

Note that the walking minutes and the driving miles shown on the charts do not always tally with those in the text; the charts usually show round numbers.

Note also that I sometimes take you along canal towpaths. These are not normally public rights of way, and you walk there by courtesy of the owner of the canal.

At the end of each route, there are suggestions about getting to the next. The routes are usually close together; by road the whole distance from Edale to Ilkley Moor is less than 75 miles.

On principle nothing is second-hand in this book. I have taken advice from numbers of people, but almost everything I recommend (and *all* the routes) I have tried myself, usually many times.

The character of the walks varies, one advantage of the Pennines is that they make this possible. You can go for the wild and purely rural, like route one, or the mixed urban and rural with places to visit on a wet day like route three. The buildings also change, as you move further north you see more of the typical squat windows of the Pennines.

The walks can be treated as you please. There and back in a day if you are energetic, or each one spread over a week if you have a young family. Most of the routes pass playgrounds where the younger children can have a change from the walking. Each will take you through scenery where you can see nature at its most varied, from the woodlands and the thick vegetation of the valleys to the dark peat and the heathers of the moors. You can also see how people have travelled and struggled in this hard country for centuries. Some of the relics portray craftsmanship and vivid imagination, others contain harsh reminders of human greed and cruelty.

You will see a wide selection of living things – plants, animals, birds, insects. Some that you may like to look out for are mentioned on these pages, but of course there are many more. This book is an entertainment not an encyclopaedia. If you are a bird expert you will know that about 80 different species can be seen on the moors and in the valleys. I have chosen some which make a special contribution to the local life and which it may amuse you to try to identify; but I only mention those I have seen myself. Other living creatures as well as plants and human relics are treated in the same way. On some of the walks almost every stone and every building can tell a story. So I have had to be choosey, and leave out many things you might like to know, while spelling out a few legends.

The idea is to provide some walking, and some stopping and looking. This is a holidaymaker's companion – trusty but not too demanding. You may be the typical family I have in mind, or you may be the leader of a group excursion, or you may be on your own. In case you have companions who get bored, some guessing games are suggested – a quiz can be made up out of almost every page in the book and many of the marks on the landscape; and there is a quiz at the end of the book to test your powers of observation. If you want to make any comment or to ask a question why not drop me a line?

The address is 21 Barnfield, Urmston, Manchester M31 1EW; please enclose a stamped and addressed envelope. If you are into the new technology send me an MBX via Telecom Gold: 72 MAG 20263, or Prestel:61748768.

Walking about in someone else's workshop

There are some things to settle before we start. One is a necessary reminder, not to you, of course, but to all the other readers. The Pennine hills, like every other holiday area, are a playground to some and a workplace to others. In your office or factory or school, or whatever, you do not usually have to put up with strangers climbing in through the windows, overturning the chairs or strangling one of the staff. Perhaps you would be glad if that did happen; but the farmer is not glad when a sheep is suffocated by chewing a plastic bag or a precious dog is lamed by stepping on an empty can. Nor is he pleased to find a gate broken or a wall knocked down. The hill farmer has to work a lot harder than you do, I guess, and for less money. A shepherd in these hills walks about 30 miles a week, and the uphill half of the walking adds up to the height of Everest at least 9 times a year. He can do without the problems caused by thoughtless tourists, when a new gate costs about £150 (always shut it unless it is actually fastened open), and to repair one yard of stone wall can cost about £10.

So why not go a little further than just avoiding damage? Why not replace the stone that someone else has knocked off? A companion and I were once helping a farmer who was struggling to dig out his snowbound landrover when a strong-looking and well-equipped hiker walked past offering no more than a condescending smile by way of help. But do not try to be too helpful, let the sheep look after themselves. They know how to care for themselves better than you do, even when they appear to be in trouble. And never let your dog off a lead when there are sheep around. The most obedient city-trained dog can forget himself in the heady Pennine air, and can cause a sheep to fall over a precipice when he is only being playful and intending no harm.

There are small firms all over the hills engaged in various activities like quarrying or mining, engineering, scrap dealing and haulage as well as textiles, clothing and shoes. The people who run these firms are hard-working individualists who have little time for public relations, still less for visitors who only want to gape at them, and none at all for trespassers. The place to meet them is in the pub after work, not in their own backyard just after you have scrambled over a fence you imagined to be derelict. I was once challenged by a young child after I had strayed – by mistake, naturally – off the path. To the fierce enquiry about what I thought I was doing there, I meekly replied that I was looking for a Roman fort marked on my map. 'Oop there', said the primary school security man pointing to a nearby hill. His directions,which included walking through a cricket ground were so clear and precise that I had walked for ten minutes before I realized that I had been hoaxed – there was no place for a cricket ground among the local contours.

The higher ground is often shown on the map as 'open country'. There are signs to tell you that you can walk anywhere except when grouse-shooting parties are in possession. The days are clearly marked, are very few in the course of a year, and never include Sundays, so do respect the rules. You do not have to like other people's hobbies, any more than they have to approve of yours, but there does have to be mutual tolerance. If you have a problem, the answer is to read the notices. There are also areas where access is forbidden at all times even on footpaths; the Ramblers' Association is campaigning against the forbidden areas right now.

I was once leading a party of apprentices frcm Sheffield on one of the walks described in this book. Part of the exercise was to make sure that the lads learnt how to behave in the countryside. So we read the notices and knew there was no shooting that day and that we were in an area where access was permitted; but we met a shooting party all the same. Of course we tried to keep out of its way, and it was no help at all when a deer stalker hat on top of a tweed suit came bounding across the peat and yelled at the boys. He attacked, as it were, our left flank and I was on the right, so I had no chance to point out to him that the words he used did not fit any of those present except himself, and more than undid all my efforts to teach care of the countryside.

My complaints to the local authority produced the following information:

– that the agreement not to shoot except on the days mentioned was only a voluntary one, nevertheless the owners thought it was being kept;
– that the source of the trouble was a gamekeeper who was running his own private shooting parties on his days off;
– that we would need to be experts on shooting to know how to keep out of the way once a party was in sight.

So that was all right, then.

Before reaching the open country signs, it is essential to keep to the paths otherwise you are sure to trample on something that is precious to someone. The farmer and nature between them make the countryside a pleasure to walk in, neither are much good on their own. Did you know, for instance, that if the sheep disappeared much of the area would become impassable? They help to keep the paths open for you; but at the same time over-walking is making some of the paths dangerous and measures have to be taken to preserve them.

For nature, too, the rule is *do not touch. Never* pick wild flowers – someone else has the right to enjoy them too – catch insects or raid birds' nests. Did you know that there are 80 species of birds in Britain for whom it is a criminal offence even to photograph their nests without a permit? If you want to study nature, let me propose your local college of further education. If you have no time for that, please be content to observe and enjoy without interfering. The same applies to collecting treasures from the earth. Archaeology is a skilled business where the blundering amateur can do much harm. Too many magpie visitors collect birds' eggs or fossils or Roman remains.

A guidebook writer of 100 years ago wrote about tourists rolling stones from a wall down a hillside, Sunday school teachers on an outing bickering about who had picked the best flowers and someone showing off a collection of birds' eggs on a local railway station. At least he did not have to grumble about the litter in those days. Writing about the top of Kinder Scout (route one), I have been tempted to say that you could follow the most difficult part of the route by the plastic bags and drink cans. On a 2,000 foot high peat plateau, with no roads anywhere near, these can only have been left by hikers.

Possibly the worst vandal of all is the motorist who digs up patches of grass on the moors to take home to repair his lawn. That is a particularly mean form of theft to save a few pennyworth of seed; the grass stolen took a lot of nature's ingenuity to grow in that inhospitable soil.

Safety

While you are looking after the interests of nature and the farmers, do look after yourself as well. Even in the South Pennines, which are nowhere near as dangerous as the Lake District mountains, there are plenty of traps for the unwary. Watch for the sudden change of weather or the treacherous bog or rock. The Mountain Rescue Parties, all volunteers, have to cope with too many calls as it is.

One cold winter's evening I met a young family – Mum, Dad and three children under twelve – on Kinder Scout, a mountain you will find yourself climbing on route one. My companion and I, who thought we knew every inch of the ground, had temporarily missed our way through the fog and the snow; but this family had never been in the district before. There were one and a half miles of darkness to add to the fog and snow between them and their car, and they were going in the wrong direction. If we had not met them, they could have made headlines – 'Frozen corpses in Sunday suits.'

How to get there

About a seventh of the population of Britain lives within an hour's drive of the South Pennines. So eight million people can manage these routes from home. For the rest this is an ideal holiday area, so long as you do not need the seaside and your children enjoy the hills. It is especially ideal, if that's English, for the small party. And allow me to let you into a secret: nearly 7,999,000 of the eight million never come near so there is still plenty of room among the nation's most neglected beauty spots.

Each chapter includes a note on the public transport and the roads to the area described. You can approach through Sheffield, Huddersfield, Bradford or Manchester; the two last routes (Brontë country and Ilkley Moor) are partly within the City boundaries of Bradford and all the routes have direct access by public transport from Manchester. For cars, the M62 goes through the middle of the region – four of the routes are to the north of it and three to the south.

Equipment

The message of this book is: don't despise these hills. They make marvellous friends and vicious enemies. All of which adds up to warm and windproof clothes, and one more piece than you think you are going to need. Also required are strong, waterproof, *walking* boots. If you are not an expert, take advice on the boots and be sure to get them large enough for *two* pairs of socks.

No maps are printed in this book (the charts are crude sketches to show times and distances); you need proper maps and that means Ordnance Survey. Every inch of the routes described are shown on the 1:50,000 series sheets 103, 104, 109, 110. Your local bookshop will know the jargon if you do not, but order soon; there is always one out of stock when you want four. All except routes three and seven can also be followed on the 1:25,000 Leisure Series: no.1 the Dark Peak and no.19 the South Pennines. The smaller sheets of the 1:25,000 Pathfinder Series are also worth having, but you need to carry plenty as you soon walk off one.

At the beginning of each route I have given a 'grid reference'. If you are not familiar with this method of finding places on a map, this is how it works. Edale station (route one) is 122 853. To find it you look for the line going north-south (up and down the map) numbered 12 and move two tenths of the way towards line 11. You then find east-west line 85 and move three tenths of the way up towards line 86. The place where 122 and 853 cross is Edale station on either of the recommended maps. The system is fully described on the 1:25,000 Leisure Series Maps.

In addition to the maps and the clothes you will need the standard equipment for all hill walking:

- a first aid case,
- a container of water,
- a whistle (but *only* to be used in emergency),
- emergency rations,
- a compass,
- a torch.

If you want to know more about recommended equipment, read *The Walker's Handbook* by H.D. Westacott, published by Penguin. The book on the Pennine Way I mentioned is: *Pennine Way Companion* by A. Wainwright, published by the Westmorland Gazette.

Eating, shopping and sleeping

The towns along these routes – apart from Haworth which is in a different class, see route six – show signs of the early stages of *touristalization,* the holiday-making equivalent of industrialization. At this stage barns are converted into restaurants and craft shops take over old mills, but bed and breakfast signs are still scarce. And that means do not outwalk your strength. Pub grub is now usually available seven days a week (at least at mid-day), but take emergency rations just in case.

Stop before you need to and look around for somewhere to stay the night. If you are near the Pennine Way, the hostels and guest houses that do exist may be fully booked in the summer. Information centres will give advice on accommodation (you can phone and ask as soon as you plan to come), so will the Yellow Pages if you can find them in post offices or phone boxes. Most of the area comes either in the Manchester (North), Sheffield, Huddersfield or Bradford directories, and each chapter in this book tells you the exchanges to look out for. You will need to search under hotels or guest houses, because the compilers have never heard of bed and breakfast and to them the word 'Accommodation' is used for an address you have your letters sent to if you do not want your spouse to see them. *Farms* do exist in the yellow pages, but the farmer entry gives no idea which offer bed and breakfast, and phoning round them all is not recommended. What the farm entry does is to provide fine entertainment for a wet afternoon. Top-o-th-Knotts, Three Lovers and Woos Nab can all be found in half a column of telephone directory under 'farms'.

One other word about telephoning round for somewhere to stay – keep a pocket full of coins. A promise to "fetch me mam" may mean a long wait. Like you she's always in the bathroom when the phone goes. Not that you will often be milking the cows, which was the excuse given by the landlady of one *pub* I called.

Two kinds of eating place are recommended – the hiker food of the pub or small cafe and the restaurant meal. Obviously the word 'good' means good of its kind. The pub grub is often excellent; the visitor who wants to dress up and go out for the evening will find plenty of possibilities but few centres of gastronomic pilgrimage. That is natural enough, the most discriminating eaters look for their favourite cholesterol supplies·in the nearby cities. Words like 'rip off' spring to mind when a dose of ill-chosen steak accompanied by some fast unfrozen additives brings a bill of over £10 per person. So check before you enter that picturesque barn.

I have no desire to get into the reataurant-guiding rat-race, but a few suggestions are made here and there. I can honestly say that standards are going up, but conditions change quickly. One of my favourite restaurants deteriorated after a change of ownership and has been left out; others have improved. Many of the restaurants make up in position and attractiveness what they lack in cooking. The suggestions made in each chapter are to help you to choose an eating place without making a too expensive mistake and without straying too far from your route. Ownership changes frequently and there may be further changes by the time you read this; but those I recommend I have really enjoyed. I never mention a place I have not visited myself. I have not necessarily stayed overnight in all of them, but I have looked at the bedrooms, and I always check the loos; if the loo's dirty, the kitchen is likely to be dirty too.

Those who earn large salaries by hoodwinking us put around stories like 'you get what you pay for.' This is frequently untrue, in my experience, but especially in restaurants. Of course you will not get a gourmet meal for the price of fish and chips at a takeaway, but a meal at about £8 can turn out better than one for which £15 is charged. On most routes, I have recommended one restaurant which provides excellent meals at a price which seemed fair for the quality. I have recommended no restaurants where the staff are unfriendly or smoke on duty, or where there has been an obvious defect in the food or service. I have been less fussy about the pubs if they are in handy positions, but I have noted the excellent ones which, in addition to tasty food, cleanliness and attentive service provide a good meal including jacket potatoes or rice as well as chips.

Souvenir shops are called craft shops in these parts, that can make them expensive and yet not so individual as you might expect. Some are excellent, as are some little art shops and specialized jewellers. The main shopping centres are at Hebden Bridge and Ilkley, but watch out for the small shop in the unexpected place.

Those words

The author has walked, cycled and driven many times over the area described. Take it for granted that everywhere I suggest is marvellous, beautiful (with a 'rugged sort of beauty', of course), unsurpassed, fascinating, wild and peaceful You would not be going there otherwise, would you? Take it for granted, too, that those words will not be used on these pages. I assume that you will notice the everyday stuff of guidebook jargon for yourself and just need me to show you around.

Nor will I usually tell you whether the walks are 'tough' or 'easy' – other people do that to impress you with their virility, I suspect. I assume that what I can do you can do also. Personally I find that the toughness of a walk varies with how I feel. If I have been working at my desk non-stop for six weeks trying to meet a publisher's deadline, any walk is tough; once I am back in training again, the same walk seems easy. What I do is to warn you against doing too much at once, about the dangerous parts especially in the first three walks, and about stretches that are unsuitable for young children.

The Quiz

At the end of the book is a quiz to entertain you. As part of the quiz there is an intentional mistake in each route; the mistakes are quite obvious, but you will not lose your way if you miss them.

And those booklets

Every tourist information centre in the area, and many of the pubs and cafes, sell booklets – local history, walks, natural history and so on. So do the museums and libraries. Some are fascinating, some are boring. Those listed at the end of the chapters are ones I have enjoyed reading, but new ones are appearing all the time, so keep your eyes open.

The *Pennine Magazine* (bi-monthly) is full of fascinating, informative and colourful detail and is available all over the area. You will not believe this when you see it, but it is edited and written by volunteers – an outstanding example of professionalism among volunteers.

Other magazines about life in the area are: *The Dalesman, Yorkshire Ridings Magazine, Yorkshire Life* and *Lancashire Life*.

Finally note that many of these walks take you in a straight line, I know that many hardened hikers make a habit of always walking round in circles and I have included circular walks too. Personally I like to retrace my steps – you always see a totally new angle on a piece of countryside when you approach it from the opposite direction. In any case, you can always return by public transport, or a lift from the carbound members of the family if you do not want to walk back.

Enjoy yourself, breathe that Pennine air, and be fit.

Route 1:

Edale, Kinder Scout and Hayfield

The maps for this route are: Ordnance Survey Outdoor Leisure Series (1:25,000) no. 1, The Peak District, Dark Peak Area; Ordnance Survey 1:50,000 series no. 110, Sheffield and Huddersfield. The grid reference for Edale station is 122853 and for the Quarry at Hayfield, 048869.

There is a visitor centre at Edale (Peak Park Ranger Service), phone 0433 70207, and at Hayfield: 0663 46222 (Derbyshire Country Ranger Service).

Edale is our starting point; a group of four small hamlets nestling under Derbyshire's highest mountain, Kinder Scout, it is a paradise for walkers. All the signs show that hiking is the main industry here, but there are other outdoor sports as well.

Like most places in this book, Edale has a long past. Tools made over 10,000 years ago have been found in these hills. Apparently the hunting season was different then: the tools are thought to have been left by summer visitors. I prefer the place in winter, there is someone else here in summer; but do not let that put you off, there is always plenty of room.

Edale just missed a very different present. Samuel Fox, a nineteenth century wire drawer from the Hope valley, nearly started a steel industry in the area. In fact he moved a few valleys north to Stocksbridge, an area that was for farming only in his time, and founded what has now become a mighty steelworks. Since then both an oil-field and a reservoir have been suggested, but neither has happened.

Hayfield, the other place we are visiting, is larger. An old agriculture centre – once boasting a huge May Fair of sheep and cattle - it turned itself into a textile centre, first wool and later cotton; it also turned from cottage industry to mills. It is claimed that the folk song 'Come Lasses and Lads' originated in Hayfield. More recently the famous television actor Arthur Lowe (of Dad's Army fame) lived here until his death.

During the last war a German bomber crashed into Kinder Scout; numerous other airplanes crashed in this area during and before the war.

While in Hayfield, have a look at the church. The first church on the site was built 600 years ago (in 1386), and the present building is really well kept inside, with bright painting and a little lobby partitioned off where they were serving coffee the last time I looked in. Seldom do you see a church so obviously cared for. And when you come out of the church, take a walk along by the river. There are some seats on the edge where you can watch the water splashing over the rocks, enjoyed by large ducks with unusual mixtures of white, brown and black with dashes of red.

Between Edale and Hayfield is Kinder Scout, the mountain into whose ample breasts Edale snuggles. Kinder Scout is not just a pretty hill – it is a whole plateau (five square miles of it) with numbers of little rocky peaks and a network of valleys breaking up the brown peat – with its beauty and its menace. The name of this mountain will recur many times; it dominates this chapter.

There are higher mountains further north – and further west in Wales – but at just over 2,000 feet it is the highest in Derbyshire. It stands in the Dark Peak, an area where the rocks are millstone grit (so-called because they make good grinding stones) in contrast to the White Peak – the limestone area further south. And it provides real mountain-walking, not just hiking on hills.

Edale claims three firsts to mark it off from the other places you will visit:

– the first purpose built national park visitor centre, built by the country's first national park authority, was opened here;

– the first national park warden patrols started here on Good Friday 1954, now called ranger patrols;

– the first of the network of long distance footpaths, the Pennine Way, was officially opened here on 24 April 1965.

To get to Edale

By train: Infrequent trains from Manchester and Sheffield, with good connections from further afield.

By bus: Only on Summer Sundays and Bank Holidays.

By road: From Sheffield, the A625 (turn right at Hope, signpost Edale).

From the M1, south, leave at exit 29, then: A617 to Chesterfield, followed by the B6051 which joins the A625 between Sheffield and Hathersage. From M1, north, leave by junction 36 and follow A61 towards Sheffield, then A625.

From Manchester or Derby, follow the A6 to Chapel-en-le-Frith and then the A625 to the Edale signpost (left near top of hill).

If you must come by car, do come early. I counted 115 cars *outside* the car parks one Sunday in May!

To get to Hayfield

By public transport: buses from Stockport and Manchester, New Mills or Glossop. At all these places it is possible to change from a train.

By road: Find the A6, then: from the south turn right on to the A624 at Chapel-en-el-Frith and keep on this road (watch where it turns right by the railway, on the outskirts of Chinley); from the north turn left onto the A6015 (signpost New Mills). From Sheffield follow the A57 to Glossop and then turn left onto the A624.

Note: If you come by car, make for the quarry car park (less than a mile east of the town) and come early. There is a much larger car park by the information centre just east of the town (with a pedestrian subway under the bypass).

Food, accommodation and shopping

(The telephone exchanges to look for in the yellow pages are Hope Valley for Edale and New Mills for Hayfield.)

Edale (population 320) is a tiny place and very popular, it deserves to be. 46,000 people called at the information centre last year, so well over 100,000 must have visited the village. Which means: do not arrive at midnight on a summer Saturday expecting to find accommodation without difficulty. There are a number of bed and breakfast places, farms and hotels; ask at the helpful information centre. They can provide details but cannot make bookings; they are not that sort of information centre. Among the hotels is The Rambler (used to be called 'The Church'), situated by the station and owned by the Ramblers Association. Apart from a long hike from bedroom to bathroom, it is reasonably comfortable. Ask for room 1 if you like ghosts, or for rooms 5 or 6 if you are a train spotter.

The Rambler Inn.

There is also a youth hostel, about which more later, and numerous camp sites. Whether you favour tents or caravans the neighbourhood is covered with places to pitch or park.

For food and drink there are two pubs (the Rambler and the Old Nag's Head), which serve reasonable food – you have an alternative to chips in both – and good beer. The Nag's Head has the atmosphere and the Rambler has the space. There are also two cafes, one at the station and one at a camp site in the centre of the village.

For souvenir shops, go to Castleton.

Hayfield is a larger place altogether and has a selection of pubs, small cafes and bed and breakfast accommodation. It also has one gourmet restaurant for that special night out – The Skillet Restaurant, Steeple End Fold. Right on the route is the Sportsman (on Kinder Rd near the quarry car park) with fine food (the best chilli con carne I tasted in the South Pennines) and beer, also accommodation (with private facilities) and a restaurant. There are regular jazz nights. In the middle of Hayfield is an unusual pub, the Royal, which started life as a vicarage; the building has changed its character more than once. There is food, drink, accommodation and a warm welcome here as well as the token ghost. Inside is a marvellous collection of photographs of old Hayfield, including the building of the Kinder Reservoir. Outside the pub is a cricket pitch. Back in 1931, the town had a flood of such violence that the roller was washed off the pitch.

Sports and hobbies

Edale and Hayfield are famous for hiking and camping, but there is much else to do. You can try skiing (sometimes), rock-climbing and shooting (if you can afford it). Nearby is Losehill Hall, an open air pursuits centre owned by the National Park Authority, and the National Trust run regular work camps here. There is potholing not far away.

Both the pubs at Edale have notices *encouraging* hikers – elsewhere in the South Pennines they are likely to be tolerated rather than encouraged – and Kinder Scout is an exception to the rule of so many hilly areas in Britain that you are on your own once you have walked 50 yards from a car park.

The Youth Hostel (0433 70302) was once a rich industrialist's country house, two miles east of the village (towards Hope and Sheffield). It employs a full-time instructor in outdoor pursuits. You are offered canoeing, climbing, folk (and other music), hill walking, horse-riding, keep fit, map and compass tuition, natural history and numerous other activities. Near the youth hostel is a pony trekking centre.

The Youth Hostel has family rooms and caters for all ages; the Chestnut Centre (0625 878980), a few miles west of Edale near the town of Chapel-en-le-Frith, offers a nature trail (owls, otters, badgers, foxes and much else), but its speciality is providing activity holidays for children apart from their parents. Activities, include abseiling, archery, camping, canoeing, caving, climbing, horse-riding, nature studies and swimming.

An even wider variety of facilities, for young and old, is provided at Losehill Hall (0433 20373), the National Park Study Centre, near Castleton.

At Hayfield you can find most of the sports already listed plus fishing. The town is also rich in pub games – pool, draughts, dominoes and darts – with competitions between pubs. There is live music in some of them.

Special sights and events

Sheepdog trials are held in the Hope Valley.

Castleton caves. In nearby Castleton, there are numerous caves open to visitors (one is visited by boat). Here is mined a unique mineral, Blue John, which makes colourful vases (blues, purples, white and blacks) and is found nowhere else – vases made of Blue John were dug up in the ruins of Pompeii. There are also opportunities for potholing in the area.

Castleton garlanding. A procession and decorating of the Church tower with a huge oak garland by a horseman in Stuart costume takes place at the end of May.

Edale Blue Grass Festival. On the first week in June over 1,000 people assemble at Nether Ollerbrook Farm (half a mile to the east of the village) for a national festival of Blue Grass music. In case you did not know, this is played by five piece bands, developed from old time fiddle bands in the States. To the non-blue grasser it sounds something like country music.

A well-dressing.

Hope well dressing. A distinctively Derbyshire custom (also met at Glossop on the next route) is well-dressing. A village well is decorated by a large tableau made of leaves and petals representing a biblical or other scene. You can see

18

a well-dressing somewhere in the area at almost any time between late spring and early autumn, the ceremony at Hope is held at the end of June or beginning of July.

Hayfield has a May Queen festival in the middle of May – the exact weekend, I am told, is decided each year to avoid clashing with the cup final. There is a jazz festival in late June, in which many of the pubs take part, and sheep dog trials in late September.

Safety

Travelling from central or south eastern England, Edale provides the first encounter with the highlands. The hills of Derbyshire are full of character, but they are soft and easy-going compared to those from Kinder Scout northwards. Here are real mountain conditions – a fast changing climate, often harsh, with treacherous peat and bogs, and the need to scramble up slippery, narrow paths with steep drops below. A great friend, but a deadly enemy is Kinder Scout.

Before you start out, take a look at the Church. A bland building, on the outside nothing to object to, little to admire; late nineteenth century grey, jostling with the green of a well-kept churchyard, built by subscriptions from local worthies after Edale became a separate parish. As you walk through the door, a plaque on the wall opposite rivets your attention. It bears the names of three young men – rover scouts – who died walking on the 'Four Inns Walk.'

It was Saturday, 14 March 1964 when Gordon Stewart Withers, John Butterfield, Michael Welby and 250 other rover scouts set out on a 40 mile walk from the site of a demolished pub at Holmfirth – the Isle of Skye – to the Cat and Fiddle near Buxton. It was wet but not too cold when they started; the next morning, the rain turned to snow and the moors froze under a bitter wind. Stewart, a local lad, was found on the Sunday evening, unconscious. He died in hospital. The bodies of the other two (who were from the south) were found near Alport river (see route 2) after rescuers had forged a way through mountainous snow drifts.

Do not underestimate these mountains. The local rescue teams are called out to 70 incidents a year, usually less dramatic than that fatal Four Inns walk; but all meaning pain and hardship for rescuers as well as rescued and relatives.

Many of the casualties are climbers, but the walkers are usually those without sufficient clothes (some of those rover scouts wore shorts), sufficient food or sufficient knowledge of how to get around.

But cheer up. With this book, a map, a compass, some good companions and the clothes and food, the danger adds spice. Only be sure it is your danger not everyone else's.

So let's start

I am offering you more choice on this route than the others, because the area is a natural for hikers. I am also taking you along some of the Pennine Way, although I promised to keep off it in the last chapter – it just is the safest way to see Kinder Scout and that must not be missed. You can take dogs, on leads of course, because most of the stiles are not too difficult except for one section which can be avoided; but very young children can only be taken on the first walk, that is why I place it first.

Walking route A: Ringing Roger and Grindsbrook

Remember: there is an intentional mistake on each of these walking routes, see the quiz at the end of the book.

Start from the station and turn left, the car park is just across the road; walk along the road, northwards towards the village, the information centre is on your right after the first *5 minutes*. It provides a mine of information on the area including a display of mountain rescue equipment and how not to need it. In another *5 minutes* you reach the Old Nags Head. Follow the track that passes to the left of the pub and eventually leads into a footpath that crosses a wooden bridge through a copse and onto open country the other side. Soon after you emerge, *10 minutes* from the Old Nags Head, a path turns off to the right. This leads up to Ringing Roger which takes about half an hour. It is ideal for the very young family – I have seen a four year old climb it unaided – because it provides plenty of scrambling without serious dangers.

If you turn right when you rejoin the main path after coming down from Ringing Roger, you follow up Grindsbrook Clough, a path you will be coming down on the second route in this chapter. You could be at the top in about *an hour and a half*. In the stream you follow, you will see a number of small dams. These were built here, as elsewhere in these hills, to wash sheep in the days before modern sheep dips.

On your return you can see the skyline to the south east (beyond Edale). The nearer hill is called Lose Hill, and the one to the left of it with the truncated mound on top, Win Hill. Legend has it that two armies faced one another on these hills in prehistoric times; the army that won the battle camped on Win Hill.

Ringing Roger.

Walking route B: Edale, Kinder Scout and Hayfield

(Compass essential)

This is an ambitious walk, through some of the finest scenery in Britain; it takes you over some rough and stormy places, but there are plenty of chances to turn back.

Follow the road from the station to the Old Nags Head *(10 minutes)* and then turn left. Do get the turning right; it's *not* the one to the shop and camp site, but the next. There are two footpath signs. One reads 'Barber Booth and Hayfield' and the other is the Pennine Way (wet weather) sign. On the gate is a memorial to one Ray Meynell, 'for services to rambling.' Perhaps someone will put up a plaque to me: 'for services to the Department of Transport,' you will find out why later.

After *5 minutes,* turn left at a stile (footpath sign to Hayfield) and follow the path across a meadow. Four stiles and *15 minutes* later, you continue upwards to another signpost (this one reads 'open country', most confusing these footpath signposts). In *2 minutes* you keep slightly left, through a gap in a wall and follow a path down between high grassy mounds over the next stile *(3 minutes),* across a meadow and over yet another stile *(2 minutes).* The path is indistinct, but you cross diagonally a corner of one meadow and most of the next after passing through a gap in a hedge (a change from a gap in a wall) marked by a yellow painted stone and in another *2 minutes* cross to another stile in the far corner of the field.

You will have passed a number of sheep by now, and will obviously be wondering what breed they are. The majority are Swaledales. They have curly horns and black faces and are common elsewhere, but there are two local breeds as well. The sturdy looking little creatures with black faces but no horns are Derbyshire Gritstone; those with horns and white faces are another local breed called Woodlands Whiteface.

In *4 minutes* follow the path through a farmyard and turn right onto a small road (there is a phone box here in case you need it). Follow the road past signs to open country, the Pennine Way and Jacob's Ladder and in *10 minutes* arrive at Lee Farm. Here is a converted barn called 'Information Shelter', an imaginative idea with interesting posters and a place to retreat to if you hit bad weather.

Along the way from here are signs of moorland reconstruction work by the National Trust – thousands of boots like ours have eroded the sensitive soil.

20 minutes after leaving Lee Farm, cross the packhorse bridge at the foot of Jacob's Ladder. Note the carefully designed and rounded little bridge just wide enough to take a horse and with sides low enough to avoid damaging the packs. You will see more packhorse bridges in later routes. Across these bridges and along the trails, there would be processions of merchants carrying cloth and wool on heavy laden horses – the origins of the textile trade in this country.

Three ways up Jacob's Ladder face you as you cross the bridge – to the left the old packhorse route, in front the ladder scramble, now forbidden, and to the right the modern staircase built by the National Trust and shown in the picture.

25 breathless minutes later you are near the top of the pass and the path divides.

You have now been walking for nearly *two hours* and face three choices.

Fork left and go on to Hayfield (a long way, if you have to return, but you can stop the night or come back by bus and train).

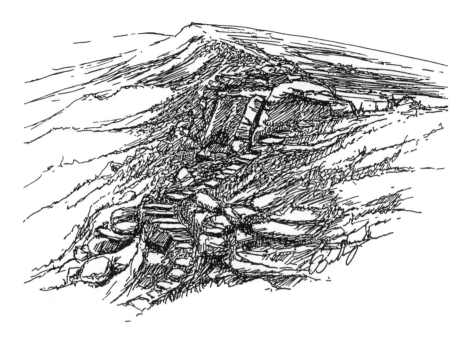

Jacob's Ladder, a path to the sky.

Fork right for Kinder Scout (allow *5 hours* to be on the safe side, less in really fine weather).

Turn back and follow the way you came up with a totally different view of the valley (it will take just over *an hour* back to Edale station).

If you decide to fork right, follow the path up the side of the hill; once past a small peak on your left, leave the path and cross a short piece of rough ground going northwards (obliquely left from the path). Soon you will pick up a track taking you to the top of the peak in front of you. This is Kinder Low, one of the high points of the plateau. There is an ordnance survey trigpoint (triangular concrete post) on top; find that and you will know you are going the right way *(20 minutes* from right fork).

Walk along the rocks, still northward, the path is indistinct at first, but soon becomes clear and takes you along the edge of the plateau with a view across

Hayfield and into the Cheshire Plain. After *30 minutes* you reach Kinder Downfall, where the river Kinder pours steeply down, between heavy, carved grey rocks. The river soon rises and falls – it may be dry or it may be a torrent when you see it, and thereby hangs a tale of water supply in this wet area. These hills have little natural storage and the rain just drains off and out to sea as soon as it falls. That is why a city like Manchester can have a reputation for rain and for water shortages at the same time. The water supply cannot be pumped up from natural reservoirs, as in London, but has to be stored by man-made dams. I talked to the proprietor of a hotel high in the hills on another route who had had to deepen his well in spite of a wet summer. Below you is one of the reservoirs – the Kinder – all along the routes you will see these dams, many of them built laboriously in the last century, some of them burst to cause disastrous floods (as in Sheffield, which is not on these routes, or Stalybridge which is).

The beginnings of Kinder Downfall.

From Kinder Downfall walk delicately on the grey rocks. Here, a few years ago, a young man slipped. When he was found by the mountain rescue teams, he was fast between two boulders, shocked and in agony with several broken bones. He was eventually winched up to a helicopter. Picture it as you stand there, and marvel at the skill of the pilot who managed to avoid hitting the rocks with his rotor blades. He did avoid them and the victim, in hospital in 15 minutes, eventually recovered. Without the helicopter, it would have taken five hours and he would probably have been dead on arrival.

As you came along you will have seen many rocks which have been sculptured by the weather over millions of years in these ancient hills. Some have been compared to Henry Moore's efforts, many look uncannily like parts of the human body – you can decide which parts. One group between Kinder Low and Kinder Downfall, I call the checkmate, since they look like a group of chessmen. Others have been called frogs, toadstools and boxing gloves.

From Kinder Downfall, turn right up the bed of the Kinder river for *20 minutes* until it peters out. There are cairns most of the way. You then scramble onto the top of the peat and follow the most difficult walking in this book up and down the hillocks of peat, almost guaranteeing to get water inside your boots even in the driest weather. Follow south east, but slightly south of east until you can see a peak with an upright stone in front of you. Aim at this (there is a large rock on your right that looks like an H with rounded sides – do not get any nearer to that). When you have crossed the plateau, find a path that goes along the far side. Do not take the first valley down, it is very steep. The second, Grindsbrook Clough, is steep enough. You should reach this in *35 minutes* in fine weather – much longer in wet and *never* in a fog. From the rocks here you can see into Edale and the hills of the Peak District beyond. You know you have found the right gulley from the view, the wrong one twists much more. There will probably be other people around in any case. You will be following a track along which the villagers used to carry peat to burn in their homes. A song (actually written by a wartime evacuee from London) called the Old Peat Lane commemorates this. It has been sung and recorded by a local group.

Scramble down the rocks and follow the path below coming, in *50 minutes,* to a wooden bridge, the scene of another moorland reconstruction project and into a copse. From here the station is about *30 minutes,* passing the path to Ringing Roger and through the village.

But first note this copse and the wildlife in the area. The trees are sessile oaks (the leaves have stems unlike common oaks); there are also beech trees, rowans and alders (small seeds that look like mini-fircones). This tree is much planted nowadays because it grows almost anywhere and provides food for birds. In the valley, and sometimes on the moors, are the red grouse (the large dignified birds with an undignified squawk) and the tiny meadow pipits with their speckled breasts and white-edged tails. They flock aound here through all the year. There are golden plovers in summer and wheatears; with swallows lower down in the valley. I have seen a yellow hammer, adding a fresh splash of colour. Occasionally a buzzard can be seen swooping over the moors. I am told there are foxes and badgers, but I have never seen either here. What I have seen are mountain hares, black in summer and white in winter, running along the valleys between the peat on the Kinder plateau; but only high up, you seldom see them below about 1700 feet.

Mountain Hare.

You are now back at Edale if you decided to fork right just above Jacob's Ladder.

If you fork left, you follow the bridle path until you come to Edale Cross *(10 minutes)*. This medieval monument stands beside the track that was once an important trading route. Walk down on the bridleway (being reconstructed by the National Trust as I write) until you come to a gate and turn right over a stile *(15 minutes)*. There are several stiles on this route, so if you have a child that needs carrying or a heavy dog, I would stick to the bridleway. It does not take much longer. Follow an ill-defined grass path alongside a wall and a fence. After *5 minutes* cross a stile over the fence on your left, and then take the right hand path. You go up for a short distance, then downhill all the way with three more gates and three stiles *(15 minutes)* until you come to the first building. This is called Tunstead House and offers accommodation. Here you join a track which goes down to a road alongside the river Sett. You pass a reservoir, Hayfield Angling Club, and a camp site on your left and then come to the quarry car park, crossing the river by the Bowden Bridge. See chart 1.

CHART 1   THE LAYOUT AT BOWDEN BRIDGE

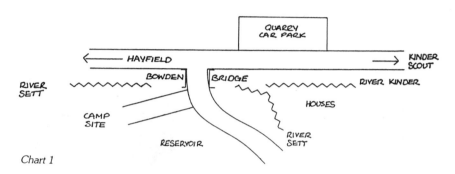

Chart 1

The quarry holds a special place in the shaky history of British liberties. What Magna Carta was to the British Constitution or Buckingham Palace railings to the suffragettes, this quarry was to the right of access to the countryside. The date was Sunday, 24 April 1932. A few hundred ramblers set out from Hayfield determined to assert their right to wander freely on Kinder Scout, then part of forbidden Britain. Earlier they had tried to show the bleak Kinder plateau to groups from the south, but had been turned back by abusive gamekeepers. This started the idea of a mass trespass. There is a memorial tablet in the quarry to prove you have come to the right place.

In the quarry the crowd was harangued by the organizers. One of them was Benny Rothman who told the story 50 years later, when over 10,000 people turned up to celebrate the jubilee and to learn that nowadays 100 miles of established footpaths are being *closed* every year.

Benny stressed that the trespassers were disciplined and orderly – one of them spent the day protecting a grouse's nest from being trampled on – but the provocation led to troubles later in the day. In the event five of the leaders went to prison, Benny among them. Those prosecuted were all under 23; this was a young person's movement frowned on by the rambling establishment, let alone the jury of country gentlemen who took no time at all to arrive at a verdict of guilty.

Launching the Kinder Trespass.

Of course there is another point of view. There were those who argued that illegal actions set back the cause, as some have always argued with illegal actions. It antagonized the landowners and made them less likely to negotiate, the critics say. There was another point of view at the jubilee celebrations, too. Access in the Peak district costs £400,000 a year and causes much suffering, like that of the ram who had his horns broken off with a hammer by a bored archaeology student. Not the sort of access the trespassers were fighting for, any more than they would have welcomed the motorbikes that now plague so much of the hills, or the litter. These trespassers mostly came from the cities; three hundred years earlier a local inhabitant struck another kind of illegal blow for freedom – by refusing to go to church.

Stand in the quarry and ponder on the struggle for liberty, whether you like the methods or not, and the twists and turns the struggle sometimes takes.

Now come back to earth, you have a big decision to take. Edale, by the route back that I am suggesting is *4 exhausting hours* away. Can you make it? One time I walked from here to Edale, it was a bright sunny afternoon when I started;

some instinct made me turn back after an hour, when I was already near the top of the pass. Luckily. I was only just back in Hayfield when a monster hailstorm blacked out the daylight.

If you do not want to return today: there is a phone box only a few minutes' walk down the road, and accommodation at the Sportsman nearby.

– or you can hurry on to Hayfield *(20 minutes)*, there are plenty of places to stay there;

– or you can go through the village and under the bypass to the bus station where you can take a bus (the bus station and information centre stand on the site of the old Hayfield train station) to New Mills and then a train to Edale;

– or you can walk to New Mills Central along the track of the old branch line that is now called the Sett Valley trail; that will take you about *an hour.* The trains only take a quarter of an hour to Edale, but they run infrequently so check beforehand. At the time of writing, the last train is just after 9.00pm (21.00 hours, I beg its pardon) on weekdays and Sundays.

If you want to complete the round trip in a day – or walk back the next day – follow the road up from the quarry turning right at the gate to a water authority gate, and then left on to a footpath. There are footpath signs at both turnings, *10 minutes.* In another *5 minutes,* left over bridge. Then continue following footpath upwards. You are walking beside Kinder reservoir. Take a look at this reservoir, it took 10 years to build and a light railway through the middle of Hayfield transported the workers and the materials (there are photos of this in the Royal).

You can see Kinder Downfall on the skyline in front of you. In windy weather, it looks as if the water is falling upwards; the wind whistling round the rocks blows up a mighty spray. In dry weather, there is often no waterfall at all. In another *25 minutes,* you reach the 'boundary of open country' sign. From here you follow the path beside the stream, which it keeps crossing and recrossing. This may cause problems in wet weather. At the top *(45 minutes)* you turn right along the Pennine Way, keeping near the rocky edge until you reach Kinder Downfall in about another *30 minutes.* From here you follow the route described earlier up the Kinder river, over the peat and down Grindsbrook to Edale.

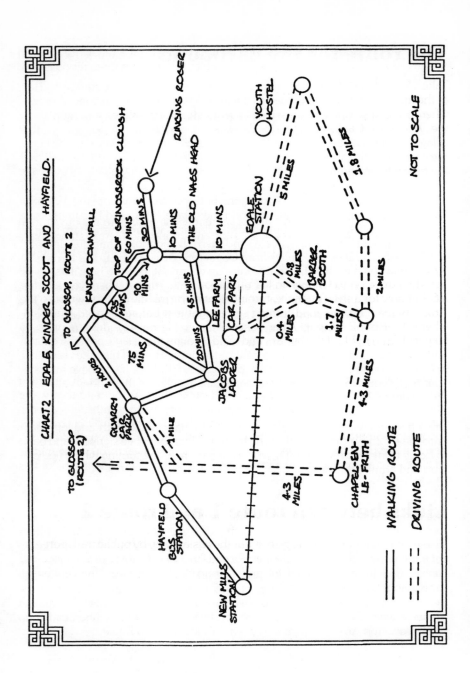

CHART 2 EDALE, KINDER SCOUT AND HAYFIELD.

RINGING ROGER

TOP OF GRINDSBROOK CLOUGH

30 MINS

KINDER DOWNFALL

TO GLOSSOP, ROUTE 2

60 MINS

10 MINS

THE OLD NAGS HEAD

10 MINS

YOUTH HOSTEL

EDALE STATION

5 MILES

2.8 MILES

35 MINS

90 MINS

45 MINS

LEE FARM

CAR PARK

0.8 MILES

BARBER BOOTH

75 MINS

20 MINS

0.4 MILES

1.7 MILES

2 MILES

JACOBS LADDER

2 HOURS

QUARRY CAR PARK

1 MILE

4.3 MILES

TO GLOSSOP (ROUTE 2)

CHAPEL-EN-LE-FRITH

4.3 MILES

HAYFIELD BUS STATION

NEW MILLS STATION

WALKING ROUTE

DRIVING ROUTE

NOT TO SCALE

The route for the carbound

Take a look at the information centre, then turn back towards the station and left at the main road. Follow this road as it winds down the valley to Hope *(5 miles)*, where you can see the well-dressing at the right time of year, then turn right along the A625 to Castleton *(nearly 2 miles)*. There is much to see in this village – Peveril Castle, which features in Walter Scott's novel Peveril of the Peak, the caves with their unusual minerals and a museum as well as the Church and the information centre.

The A625 is closed beyond Castleton, but you can drive up the Winnats Pass – fork left off the A625 just beyond the village. This road has impressive over-hanging cliffs; it is steep, but not difficult unless icy. You turn sharp right at the top (signpost 'Blue John Cavern') and then left (signpost Chapel-en-le-Frith) onto the A625. Just over *2 miles* from Castleton you pass the Edale turning. In *3 miles* you come to the Chestnut Centre on your right, do stop here if it's open. You then drive on to Chapel-en-le-Frith (another *1.3 miles)* where you join the A6, but only for a short distance, turning right in the middle of the town onto the A624. Remain on this road turning sharp right just before a speed limit sign, where the B6062 joins it. After passing under the railway, drive *3 miles* to Hayfield. Turn right off the bypass and wind through the village, past the church and over the bridge, turning sharp right onto Kinder Road. This takes you (in *1 mile)* to the quarry car park mentioned in walking route B. If you have hikers in your party, you can meet them here, and share the view of the Kinder Valley and the mountain beyond.

Drive back the way you came, turning left at Chapel-en-le-Frith and left again onto the A625. At the top of the long hill turn left at the Edale signpost and back to Edale from the other side. There is a car park near the turning where you can stop and admire the view.

Links between route 1 and route 2

These two routes are close together, but the easiest way by public transport is to get a train from Edale to Manchester (Piccadilly) and from there to Glossop. You can get a bus from New Mills if you prefer. From Hayfield there are frequent buses to Glossop.

By car, drive back to Hayfield if you are in Edale. From Hayfield to Glossop is *5 miles* along the A624.

To walk, follow the Pennine Way (starting as in walking route A) and over Kinder Scout, continuing until you reach the Snake Road, the A57, the only road you cross.

You turn left at a footpath a few hundred yards after crossing the road, and this brings you down into Glossop. Allow 7-8 hours, you can follow the road if you are behind schedule. From Hayfield there is a shorter route, turning left above the Kinder reservoir.

Booklet

A booklet I enjoyed on this area was *Kinder People* by Pam Gee. It contains no publisher's imprint, but is dated August 1985.

Route 2:

Glossop and Derwent: Doctor's Gate, the Snake and the Marching Legions:

The maps for this route are either the Ordnance Survey Outdoor Leisure Series 1: The Dark Peak (1:25,000) or Sheet 110 of the 1:50,000 Series. the grid reference for Glossop station is 034942. The information centre is beside the station, phone 04574 5920; it is not open all the time, so try to phone around mid-day. The centre is run by a private organization – the Glossop and District Environmental Council.

Glossop, the centre for this route, is a busy little town on the edge of the wildest and least inhabited moorland in the South Pennines. One area nearby is called Featherbed Moss, but don't believe it; it's next to Bleaklow which is a more accurate name. Like most of the routes, this one follows part of the course of a Roman road; but the Roman roads round here are different – you can actually see the Romans. Not that I have ever done so, but I'm told that on the night of the first full moon in autumn, the legions march again. Stationed in this area, while rebuilding an earlier wooden fort with stone, were auxiliaries from Frisia (North Holland and Germany) and Portugal as well as soldiers from Italy.

There were visitors to these parts long before the Romans. Axe heads and other remains of the middle stone age (about 8,000 years ago) have been found on Chunal Moor, to the east of the road between Glossop and Hayfield.

To get to Glossop

By train: from Manchester (half hourly, hourly on bank holidays, never on Sundays), from anywhere else change at Manchester (Piccadilly).

By bus: frequent from Manchester.

By car: from the east, the A57 from Sheffield to Manchester goes through the centre of the town. From the south, come up on the A6, turn right in the centre of Chapel-en-le-Frith onto the A624 and keep on this road to Glossop (9 miles). From the north and west, come through Manchester.

Where to stay

There are plenty of small hotels and guest houses: the list provided by the information centre gives few details, but can be seen outside the Centre when it is closed. The exchanges in the Yellow Pages directory are Glossop or Hope Valley. Three places are mentioned on the route – the Snake Inn (expensive), the Alport Barn (cheap) and the Hagg Farm Hostel (also cheap). All three need booking. The Hagg Farm Hostel is at the end of the route and is run by the Peak Park Planning Board, so you do not have to belong to any organization to stay there. The warden assures me that only two qualifications are needed – you must be alive and you must be able to pay. On principle it is open all the year round, but you are advised to phone. There is a camp site at the hostel. If you want a little luxury, try the beautifully decorated Wind in the Willows Hotel, a converted country house with a view of the Snake Road. Only a short distance from the Peak Park sign and the Ambler Memorial Bridge, the hotel stands to the south of the A57 road near the golf course.

Refreshments

There is plenty to eat in Glossop, and I have enjoyed many meals there; but I cannot look you straight in the face and say of any of the restaurants: "this provides a gastronomic experience." For shelter from the icy blast, try the Hotel Winston (in Norfolk St., opposite the railway station). It has a restaurant, bar snacks and Ruddles beer. It is comfortable, there is accommodation and children are welcome. On High Street West there is Ginger, a vegetarian restaurant, but it is not usually open in the evening; on High Street also are Indian, Chinese and Italian restaurants. There is also the Gamesley House outside the town.

Hobbies and sports

You can do almost anything in Glossop, from mini golf in Manor Park to joining in a fell race. Bird watching, bowls, fishing and sailing are among the possibilities.

You can learn to sail at the Torside Reservoir, on the B6105 which goes northwards out of Glossop to join the road over the Woodhead Pass. Near the centre of the town is a sports centre with activities that include aerobics, badminton, dance, drama, squash, swimming, table tennis; there is also a sauna, solarium and creche.

In the town are drama, opera and choral societies as well as an orchestra. Archaeologists and industrial archaeologists can find plenty of interest here. If you are a railway fanatic, you just have to come to Glossop. The Dinting Railway Centre has a great collection of steam locomotives. There are also many interesting mills around here, from the earliest down to the end of the great mill-building era at the beginning of World War I.

A cotton mill engine house.

Special sights and events

Pro Loco Festival (mid-June) when artists are invited to show their paintings and members of the public judge the winner (a similar festival is held in nearby Tintwistle).

Glossop Carnival (early July).

Melandra Castle (remains of Roman fort) just outside of the town on the main road to Manchester.

Dinting Railway Centre (preserved steam locomotives and narrow gauge trains). This is open on every day of the year except Christmas, with locomotives in steam and a narrow gauge railway that also gives rides. There is a large collection of old engines and trucks here. The locomotives include Blue Peter, which sprang to fame through the television programme; it was built in 1948 and named after a race horse. Rumour has it that this locomotive may be restored to take its turn on steam specials; but there are plenty of other fine veterans in the collection, ancient and less ancient.

Glossop Heritage Centre provides a brief but informative account of Glossop over the last seven or eight thousand years with a good picture of life in the area, especially in Roman times. When I say 'good', I mean in two senses of the word – good because it's interesting and good because it provides an optimistic view of life. The exhibition has obviously been put together by historians, genial folk who usually prefer to leave out the executions, tortures, violence, serfdom, poverty and misery which people like me notice. Ever thought of the fate of an ancient Brit caught hijacking a Roman convoy? One thing the Glossop Heritage Centre does tell you about the ancient Brits is that their queens got divorced.

The Alport Castles Love Feast. This ancient ceremony is right on the route for walkers (car drivers can just about make it). It takes place at 1.30 p.m. on the first Sunday in July.

Glossop Victorian Weekend (early September); an innovation of the 1980s with a growing reputation. I met a chap from Basingstoke who had come for the festival, and it must take something to lure chaps from Basingstoke to Glossop. Even a hardened festival-gaper like me was impressed with the scale and imagination of an event which sees the streets alive with people in Victorian costumes, plus the shop window displays, processions and sideshows; you may like to know that fortune-telling is popular in case you are in that profession.

Whitfield Well Dressing (second weekend in September, but not every year). A very ancient ceremony when a well is decorated with pictures made out of flower petals. This art form is found in many of the villages of Derbyshire; so if you arrive the wrong weekend for Glossop, you can probably find one somewhere else, see route one. The tourist information centre will advise. Another suburb of Glossop also has an occasional well-dressing.

The Local Guide lists 183 societies, so there's plenty to go at in this little town noted for its civic spirit. The list places 'Tintwistle Council of Churches' under 'Conservative Clubs', so it may not be 100% accurate; it does give you a fine range of choice from archery to fell running, from golf to skiing.

When you go to Derwent (at least 6 hours for the walkers, including stops), you can hire a bicycle, a horse, or a rowing boat (+ fishing licence), and you can rest your legs in a minibus; but you've got to get there first.

In the winter there is skiing, sledging and snow walking.

The walking route

Have a good breakfast, we've a long way to go today, but plenty of opportunities to turn back, or stop on the way, if you can't make it. Public transport does not exist on this route except on summer Sundays and Bank Holidays, so do check beforehand and please do not go too far. This is the longest and loneliest of the routes. It is a fine challenge, but be prepared to turn back or make for shelter. The chart gives the approximate times to each point. The whole way to Howden Reservoir is nearly six hours walking time, longer with stops. On summer Sundays and Bank Holidays you can get a bus from there (but not after about 6.00 pm); otherwise you still have two hours to the nearest shelter (Hagg Farm Hostel) or car park (Fairholmes).

I keep warning you not to go too far – I don't want the Mountain Rescue people round my neck, do I? – all the same I hope you will get to the end, you will see why when you arrive. So use some ingenuity, arrange to stay overnight or find a lift. This is a walk to bring out the best of the country and the best in you.

Start from the railway station, the largest car park is on the other side of the main road about five minutes walk away. Stand facing the station; an example of the best architecture in Glossop, and there's plenty of competition. Note the lion that sits over the entrance. He has walked out of the coat of arms of the Duke of Norfolk who paid for the line to be built. Then turn round in a half circle, ignore the three attractive pubs that are in vision, and walk straight ahead. This should bring you into Station Street, more or less; at the end of the street you go along a footpath which, after crossing a road, swings left between some new houses. When the path ends at a T junction, turn right and then left onto another footpath immediately after the last house. When the paths divide *(5 minutes)*, take the one on the right (there is a school on higher ground on the left). Where five paths meet take the one that goes down steeply and cross a footbridge into a park *(2 minutes)*. Take the left hand path through a children's playground and into a formal public garden with a redbrick wall on the left *(5 minutes)*. Cross another footbridge bringing you to a narrow gauge railway on your right. The park may be described as urban civilised, but of its type it is scenic with hills and valleys, a lake and a stream. Other amenities include tennis, bowls and a miniature golf course.

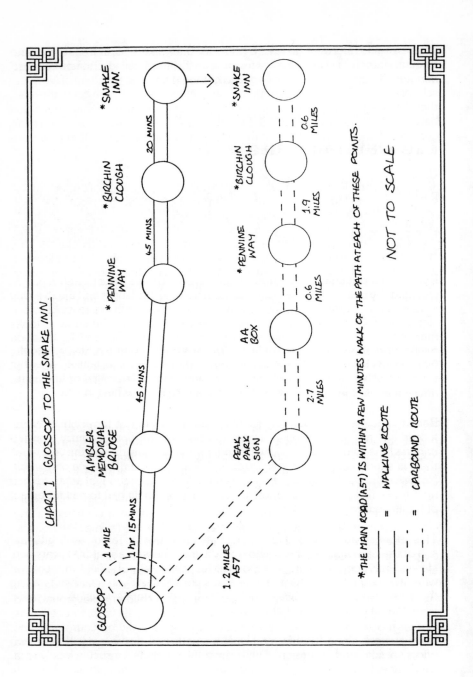

CHART 1 GLOSSOP TO THE SNAKE INN

GLOSSOP
1 MILE
1 hr 15 MINS

AMBLER MEMORIAL BRIDGE

45 MINS

*PENNINE WAY

45 MINS

*BIRCHIN CLOUGH

20 MINS

*SNAKE INN.

1.2 MILES A57

PEAK PARK SIGN

2.7 MILES

AA BOX

0.6 MILES

*PENNINE WAY

1.9 MILES

*BIRCHIN CLOUGH

0.6 MILES

*SNAKE INN

* THE MAIN ROAD (A57) IS WITHIN A FEW MINUTES WALK OF THE PATH AT EACH OF THESE POINTS.

———— = WALKING ROUTE

– – – – = CARBOUND ROUTE

NOT TO SCALE

38

After crossing the bridge follow the path that goes up the hill in front of you and through some old gate posts onto an unmade road called Church Close *(3 minutes)*. At the end of Church Close turn sharp right, past the Duke of Norfolk's school and Old Glossop parish church, and right again when you get to the road; then left past The Queen's into Shepley Street *(5 minutes)*. This brings you between two modern chemical factories (both belonging to an American company, Union Carbide). When the road turns left you continue straight ahead, to a broad path alongside a river *(4 minutes)*.

You have now moved from the old industrial, through the modern urban civilised, past some Victorian social improvement and onto modern industrialization to step suddenly out into some of the wildest countryside in Britain. All in less than half an hour. Along the path in front of you were built some of Britain's earliest factories. They have now been overrun by nature and you can hardly detect the remains.

If you can stop yourself looking round, you will see no more industry and very little else made by man – give or take the odd farm building, the fences and the shooting boxes – for the next hour or more. You will find yourself among increasingly steep slopes with snow normal until after Easter. Talking about the snow, it looks marvellous in the distance – but seen close to it soon destroys any illusions you might have about clean air. A black film demonstrates all too clearly – as the Norwegians keep saying – that we peasants from the cities are still dumping all too much of our dirt onto other people's property. This liberty will no doubt cause amazement in the future, but that future is a long time coming.

Back to the present, keep straight along the path (do not turn right over the footbridge) and pass through a gate to confront the open country sign *(10 minutes)*. As with the last walk, watch out for the very few days in the year when there is shooting. Note the steep, narrow path up to the rifle range on the left. Note also the walls where our ancestors (ours? - well, somebody's) asserted their right to a small piece of this infertile land. They probably had to pay for an act of Parliament for the privilege.

This ancient road is called 'Doctor's Gate' after a certain Dr Talbot, an illegitimate son of the Earl of Shrewsbury who was Vicar of Glossop about 500 years ago. He evidently rode this way often to visit his relatives in Sheffield to report on what was happening on their estates in his parish. Can't you hear him retailing the gossip? – Mr Buckley, he's a trusty; but Mr Brooke, now, he wants watching. We'll find an excuse to evict him."

Keep straight along the reverend doctor's path and arrive eventually at two bridges, each carefully designed with elaborate parapets for such a lonely spot. Cross the first and turn left before the second, coming to another gate

(12 minutes). A signpost tells you that this is the Roman Road via Doctor's Gate to the Snake Inn and Alport Bridge. Stop wondering whether the practical romantics who went to so much trouble to erect these signposts really thought the Romans went to the Snake Inn let alone the Alport Bridge, you've got a long way to go yourself yet.

If either the weather or you is deteriorating, you can turn back here. Cross another bridge to the right and you will soon come to a main road with a bus terminus a few hundred yards further on, a golf course too if you cannot keep away from such places. If you continue, you have left behind the last chance of a bus back on weekdays or in the winter. Very young families turn back here.

To continue, keep straight on as the Romans did, even if they did not have the Snake Inn to look forward to. You can see the hills folding into one another in front of you. Extraordinary how they manage it. The next landmark is another notice about the open country standing beside a modern barn *(10 minutes).*

One bird you should see along here is the Dipper, a small bird (just over an inch longer than your house sparrow) with a white throat and reddish brown belly. He darts, dives, flies and swims along these mountain streams all the year round. Only in winter he prefers the more sheltered canals. The person to spot one first can hand over the rucksack for the next 25 miles, give or take a mile or two. Continue along the winding valley until you come to a wooden bridge erected to the memory of Edwin E. Ambler by the Ramblers' Association and other good and worthy bodies *(15 minutes).* Near this spot, dedicated to Ambler the Rambler, you may also see the remains of a crashed aeroplane and (at the right time of year) a twisted rowan tree covered in white berries. Several planes crashed into these hills during World War II; there are photos in the Snake Inn.

From here you climb the ever-narrowing valley until you cross a stream *(30 minutes).* After this you scramble up to a narrow gorge which brings you to the Pennine Way *(15 minutes).* You can see the posts, and no doubt a number of human beings, that mark the crossing and to your right the A57 road. That gorge may look shallow on a fine day, but I have seen it full of snow to the edges on each side.

STOP and consider the past as well as your present.

A few yards before you crossed the Pennine Way, you found yourself on a stone path. These stone paths, which get even more common a little further north, are the pack horse trails. This one looks as if it had a curb, as you can see from the narrow stones that still stand upright in some places. Some of these stones appear to be inscribed. Now look along the Pennine Way as it snakes northwards between the hills. You are already on one Roman road but just out of sight – less than an hour's walking if you have the time to spare   is Shining Clough where the ghosts of the Roman soldiers still march. I cannot promise that you will see them, but if you do see some flickering lights on those moors at night do not immediately call out the rescue teams as other people have done. You might be seeing the ghosts.

Now think about yourself. You are in an exposed place with some hard walking to come, and over an hour to any shelter. You are also out of reach of public transport. Do you want to turn round, or go across to the road and either walk or thumb a lift back to Glossop, four miles away?

No? Fine. Let's go on along the path with its covering of stone which proves to be only temporary. To be followed, again temporarily, by a stretch of peat and bog *(7 minutes)*.

Note the road as it appears on your right and then disappears again into the winding valley beyond. On the left of this valley, just below the plateau, you can see the path you are making for. Take a good look, it is clearer this far away than it is close to. Your path follows alongside a small stream which soon joins a larger one *(5 minutes)*.

At the junction, cross the stream and follow the path down to the stile. You can tell you are at the right place by the National Trust sign and the signpost which reminds you, in case you've forgotten, that you have come from Doctor's Gate and Glossop. Do not cross the stile, but turn left and climb steeply up by the fence. Keep along the fence until you come down to another stream and another stile *(12 minutes)*.

Once again do not cross and do follow up by the fence. Then repeat the whole process again – down, cross stream, do not cross stile, up by fence *(8 minutes)*. There are two stiles not to cross, they lead straight down to the road. Then you come to yet another stile, but no stream this time. From here you can just make out the path you saw so clearly at a distance gradually climbing the hillside. You will also see trees below you and across the valley. When the trees come up nearly to the path *(8 minutes)*, walk to the fence and follow this to a windbreak *(6 minutes)*. Here you look down at a car park far below you which is beside a forestry commission trail.

If you are going on, cross the wind break and continue to follow the fence which protects the trees; go up the hillside and down again until you come to the next stream. You may have to go a little way upstream to cross, it is very steep by the trees, and then back to the edge of the fence *(7 minutes)*. Follow this round, and steep down, and find – wait for it – another stile you do not cross *(12 minutes)*. Unless you want to chicken out, that is, (this stile provides another chance to go down to the Snake road) follow the left hand path down. Beside this stile is the usual sign about access to open country and another signpost to the Alport Castles which is where you are going.

Think seriously before you go on. You've been out over two hours now. It's a pity to miss the Alport Castles, but you are a long way from base, unless you have stopped on the way; in winter half the daylight will soon be gone and you have no chance of public transport round here – except on summer Sundays and Bank Holidays.

You are only a few minutes from the Snake Inn; if you want a rest you can go there now.

The Snake is an old coaching house which stands about 1,000 feet above sea level. It is so far from any other pub that its mere presence must be welcome. It provides a warm shelter on a cold day; from my limited experience, I cannot recommend the beer or the bar snacks but the restaurant is good, if a bit pricy, and the service is excellent. You could stay the night; the bedrooms look comfortable, but you may have to book. One great asset the Snake has is a snack bar away from the licensed premises. The only problem is that this is never open when I am around, so I have no chance to tell you what the tea and Mars bars taste like.

Follow the path across two valleys, the first is Oyster Clough, with a stile at each end – you do cross these stiles and I hope your dog, if you have one, is a light weight or you are in trouble; continue up to a derelict shooting cabin *(15 minutes)*. Then two more stiles and a third, larger, one that takes you over a wall *(13 minutes)*. Cross a tractor path to a stone stile and pause a moment to get your breath *(4 minutes)*.

You might like to use the pause by seeing who can produce the longest list of different styles of stile. You've crossed (or not crossed) at least 4 totally different varieties in the last hour and there are some more to come. The winner can scoff the last drop out of the water bottle.

March on to the next stile, a wooden one over a wall *(5 minutes)*; after this you cross one stream and then descend steeply to another *(5 minutes)*. Then climb up to a gate and on through a second *(3 minutes)*. After this the path skirts Hayridge farm, on your right *(7 minutes)*, and joins an unmade road to Alport Hamlet *(15 minutes)*. When I first discovered the place the whole hamlet was derelict; but now life has returned, including a well restored barn where you can stay the night. The keys are available from the local farmer, but it is best to book first. This barn is the site of the ancient Alport Love Feast. You will be made very welcome, but don't get too excited; it is a religious ceremony and the loving cup

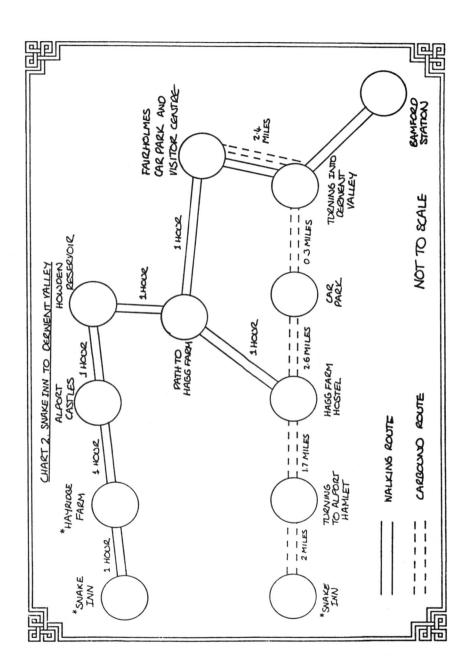

CHART 2. SNAKE INN TO DERWENT VALLEY

HOWDEN RESERVOIR

FAIRHOLMES CAR PARK AND VISITOR CENTRE

BAMFORD STATION

2·4 MILES

1 HOUR

1 HOUR

TURNING INTO DERWENT VALLEY

ALPORT CASTLES

1 HOUR

0·3 MILES

*HAYRIDGE FARM

½ HOUR

PATH TO HAGG FARM

CAR PARK

1 HOUR

2·6 MILES

*SNAKE INN

1 HOUR

HAGG FARM HOSTEL

1·7 MILES

TURNING TO ALPORT HAMLET

2 MILES

*SNAKE INN

WALKING ROUTE

CARBOUND ROUTE

NOT TO SCALE

43

only contains water. It commemorates a historic meeting when a group of ministers met in this remote spot to escape religious persecution. That was 150 years before the Snake road was built. More recently a suffragette, Hannah Mitchell, was born in the lonely farm.

After passing through a gate the path circles back on itself and brings you to a narrow wooden bridge over the river *(5 minutes)*. You then climb steeply up past one signpost to another – the open country sign again – where you are alongside the Alport Castles. *(12 minutes)*. These rock formations are not manmade. In winter, I suggest turning back here unless you have a car to meet you. This is the area where the scouts died whose memorial in Edale Church was mentioned in the last route. That is why I keep warning you.

Alport Castles.

The path continues up and over another stile *(8 minutes)* and still up *(4 minutes)*. Note the view of the Alport Castles through a narrow gorge. Once on the plateau at the top, carry on a short distance until you find a small cairn by a derelict wall *(10 minutes)*. Turn sharp right on the path to Howden Reservoir. Pass some shooting boxes with a view of the reservoir. Go through gate a into a copse where there is lush grass under the trees *(15 minutes)*.

Join a road at the point where a stream enters the reservoir *(8 minutes)*.

Take a look round. This valley survived William the Conqueror. He gave it a miss when he was laying waste Saxon England. But it did not survive the Derwent Valley Water Board. Two villages were drowned many years ago; but the water fits with the hills around.

During summer Sundays you can get a bus down the valley from here. Otherwise:

You are two hours' walk from Hagg Farm Hostel. This is clearly marked on the 1:25,000 Dark Peak map. To get there you follow the road down the valley past the first dam (the reservoir above is Howden, below Derwent) and follow the road until it does a sharp bend over a bridge. After this a path turns off to the right. This path brings you to the hostel and to the A57 main road, where you might be lucky with a lift.
   —You are *3.5 miles* from the main car park (see carbound route) —You are *6 miles* from the A57 if you keep to the road.
   —You are nearly *10 miles* (going left and first right when you reach the main road) from Bamford station.

Good luck whichever you choose.

The route for the carbound

Find the railway station. There are four roads going into Glossop and they meet at the traffic lights in the centre; there is a large pub called the Norfolk Arms standing back from the road by these lights. The station is on the left hand side of the road going north. There is a small car park here, but it is usually full. Larger car parks are at the other side of the traffic lights and on both sides of the road. On coming to the station from the lights, go straight on, up the hill, and turn right at a signpost to Old Glossop. Follow the road through Old Glossop, noting the church and other buildings of this early settlement, coming back (in about a mile) to the main A57 road, where you turn left.

The distances are short on this route, but the road is treacherous in winter and closed after blizzards. There are plenty of signs warning when it is closed, but don't take a chance when it is snowing. In summer the road is busy at weekends, but you can always find a spot to stop and admire the view.

The road twists up the narrow valley to the summit of the pass (1,680 feet above sea level and 4.5 miles from Glossop) with the scenery changing rapidly from the green of the golf course at the bottom to the sterner colours of the bare moorland on top. The hill slopes here look smooth and ulcerated at the same time. 1.9 miles further on is Birchin Clough car park, with the Snake Inn 0.6 miles after that. You can meet the walkers at either place and enjoy a glass of Britvic orange, during licensing hours of course. The word Snake has nothing to do with the shape of the road, as you might think; it comes from the Duke of Devonshire's crest. The then Duke was responsible for building the road and the pub.

In case these various Dukes are getting you confused, let me remind you. The Dukes of Norfolk dominated Glossop and their lion stands over the station. The Duke of Devonshire owned land next door; the Snake road and the Snake Inn are named after his crest. They obtained the lands by a mixture of ancient royal favours and judicious marriages, marred by a few disfavours. One Duke of Norfolk was sentenced to death by Henry VIII; he was lucky, the king died just in time, but his poet son had already been executed. You drive through several social revolutions in this book from the aristocrats to the mill-owners to the workers' cooperatives to the preservation societies.

Drive for another 1.8 miles and you will find a small track on your left, beside a farm and marked private by the Forestry Commission. This track leads to the Alport Hamlet where the Love Feast is held. After this the beginnings of the Ladybower reservoir appear beneath the all too ordered ranks of evergreens on your right. Three miles after the Alport turning is another car park. A quarter of a mile further, you turn sharp left off the main road which crosses a bridge over the reservoir. You are now following beside a branch of the reservoir which is part of a series going up this valley in which two villages were drowned by officialdom in the early years of the century. At two and a half miles the road is barred to traffic and there is a large car park with a visitor centre; there is also a place to hire bicycles. You can inspect one of the dams here. On summer Sundays there is a bus service up the valley. There are also special arrangements for the disabled.

A few yards north of this car park is an almost unbelievable stone memorial on the edge of the reservoir. It is to Tip, a sheepdog who stood by the body of her dead master for *fifteen weeks,* from 12 December 1953 to 27 March 1954, I do not exaggerate. Look north (up the reservoir) and you can just see the edge of the bleak, remote Howden Moors on which Mr. Joseph Tagg was overcome during a blizzard. Joseph was 85 years' old, well-known in the area and a winner of prizes at sheep dog trials. Don't ask me how no one managed to find him during all that time or how the dog survived (she lived off other animals overcome by the harsh weather, no doubt), but do pause a moment by this memorial.

46

The memorial to Tip.

Another monument tells you how the dam busters practised here during the war.

Return to Glossop the way you came.

Links to next route

Route 3 starts at Stalybridge.

To get there by train, you change at Guide Bridge.

To get there by car, follow the A57 back towards Manchester until the A6018 forks off to the right. Stalybridge is signposted at this point. The distance is about 6 miles.

To walk is more of a problem. The shortest and safest route is to follow the railway to Dinting and then turn left and right onto a path that goes under the viaduct and then joins the main A57 road. Walk on the pavement to the traffic lights and then straight across by a pub called the Gun. From here the paths wander around the hills but bring you to Stalybridge in a reasonable time. This route is less rural than the others and may not bring you to suitable accommodation.

You could, instead, follow the Pennine Way until it crosses the A62 at Standedge and then walk route 3 in the reverse direction; this is a long way over difficult ground, so plan carefully beforehand. You could cut out some of the difficulty by turning off the Pennine Way to Chew and Dovestones reservoirs and then to Greenfield and Uppermill (see maps).

Booklets

Glossop Heritage, published by the Glossop Heritage Committee (undated) contains a superb collection of photographs of the area over the last hundred years. *Moorland Heritage* by James S.Byford (published by the author, 1981) tells the story of the Derwent and Ladybower area, at the far end of this route. The most interesting booklet on the area that I have come across.

The Glossop Guide, published by Senior Publications, is a summary of the activities in the town and includes a street map.

You may also like to look at *Dark Peak Aircraft Wrecks* by Ron Collier, published by Wharncliffe Woodmore.

Route 3:

Stalybridge, Saddleworth, and Marsden: Abraham's chair and the packhorse trails

The maps for this route are Ordnance Survey 1:50,000 numbers 109 and 110. The grid reference for Stalybridge Town Hall is 964987. There is a visitor centre at Uppermill (phone 04577 2598) and at Marsden (0484 84602). Both can provide details of local accommodation.

We now move to a series of routes in areas where there is more public transport, so it is easier to walk short distances and return to base. This makes these routes more suitable for young families keen to stray further afield than is often possible, but no less exciting for older visitors who will find the added interest of areas soaked in history and customs.

Two pioneer crossings of the Pennines are followed by this route, a Roman road on the hills and a canal in the valley. You pass through more built up areas than on the other walks – including six small towns each with a distinctive character – and yet you often find yourself with no buildings in sight. There is a mixture of shady footpaths, industrial relics and wild moorland, with man-made lakes and waterways added to nature's steep valleys. One of the little towns, Diggle, has a Saxon name and links with their homeland will be discovered by visitors from: Belgium, Canada, Denmark, France, Germany, Italy, Netherlands, Norway, South Africa, Spain, Sweden and the United States. Most of the ancient settlers came as invaders, and those from Denmark gained a special reputation for their ruthlessness; but visitors from that country may like to know of a more peaceful connection. A nineteenth century weaver's diary says that the most popular song for singing at work was called Copenhagen. In addition to the battles of an earlier age, the area saw civil war skirmishes in the 1640s and the 1740s and riots during the nineteenth century.

This route runs in a straight line from Stalybridge in Greater Manchester to Marsden in West Yorkshire; but there are plenty of opportunities to return.

We shall follow two famous Pennine valleys – the Tame (from which the borough of Tameside takes it name) and the Colne. The six little towns that lie along the route are Stalybridge, Mossley, Greenfield, Uppermill, Diggle and Marsden. Uppermill or Diggle are suitable places for a break. These are both in the county of Saddleworth (the Post Office thinks it's Greater Manchester and the Government imagines it's Oldham, we'll settle for Saddleworth). Take time for visiting Delph where a Roman fort is being excavated. Like Diggle the name is Saxon for dig – this was a mining area over 1,000 years ago. The whole area is alive with Morris dancers on the second weekend after the first full moon in August (better check the date). They come from all over the world to join with the local experts to dance up hill and down for a whole weekend. The Saddleworth Morrismen can be seen on other weekends as well, as can the local brass bands.

How to get there by public transport

Stalybridge is a rare example of a small town with excellent rail services. Newcastle, Hull, York, Leeds, Liverpool, Huddersfield and Manchester – but not London, you are in the north now – are places with direct fast trains. From London, Birmingham and the south west you change at Stockport and from Sheffield and the Midlands at Huddersfield (but not on Sundays). From Manchester airport, you change buses at either Stockport or Manchester. There is also a network of local bus services. Phone Greater Manchester Buses for details. To return by public transport is not difficult, but do collect timetables before you start – from Greater Manchester and West Yorkshire buses as well as British Rail; you need all three. There is a bus back from Uppermill to Stalybridge, further on the buses tend to go to Oldham and you must change at Uppermill.

How to get there by road

Stalybridge is on the A635, Manchester to Holmfirth and Barnsley road. It can be reached from Huddersfield by the A62, turning left onto the A670 soon after passing over the top of the Pennines (Blackstone Edge) and left again onto the B6175 just after Uppermill, or by the A57 from Sheffield, turn right onto the A6018 at Mottram. From anywhere else take the M62 to exit 20 and follow the A627(M) to Oldham, then continue on the A627 until you reach the A635 at Ashton-under-Lyne when you turn left. Turn right off the A635 at signpost for Stalybridge town centre which brings you to the station and the start of the walk. There is not much room for parking here so you may prefer to drive on to one of the town centre car parks, but note the one-way street after you pass the station. Why not come by boat? There are moorings at Ashton basin (where the Ashton, the Peak Forest and the Huddersfield canals meet) just a mile from Stalybridge station. And if you have a canoe, you can portage it through the town and paddle parts of the route. Whether you come by land, air or water, there are plenty of chances to change your mind when you have walked enough. There are places to stay on the route, or find transport back to Stalybridge. But don't leave it too late. Accommodation and public transport are limited in these parts.

Sports and hobbies

You are going into an area famed for its sports and hobbies. If you get tired of walking you can:

- listen to a brass band (there are six of them along the route) or visit a gardening club;

fish, there are several angling societies and permits can be obtained;

- ride a horse (there are four stables in the yellow pages but more exist) or trek a pony;
- walk, run, climb, ski or orienteer;
- sail, paddle a canoe, swim, row or water ski;
- join a hang-gliding club;
- watch Morris dancing;
- race a pigeon, a whippet, a motorbike, a go-cart or a chariot;
- play pub games (readers from elsewhere may like to know that 'pool' means snooker not swimming facilities, and that 'gurning' means making faces);
- play golf, shoot (there is a range at Diggle) with rifles or bows and arrows;
- soccer, rugger and cricket pitches abound.

There is an adventure playground in Uppermill as well as plenty of other facilities for the very young. Along the route there are theatres (two and two more within easy reach), local history societies (Saddleworth has a particularly active one that runs a museum), local arts associations, photographic societies, writers' circles and a canal preservation society. Addresses change but you pass public libraries in Stalybridge, Uppermill and Marsden where you can find them. The libraries and the societies have enthusiastic staff glad to talk to visitors. The brass bands merit another word. You are coming into brass band country here, and most of the little towns along or near the route have one. They get around, too; as long ago as 1936 the Marsden Senior School Band toured South Africa; in these more affluent days the bands are struggling to survive. In Dobcross (near Uppermill) the bands have been made famous by their own historian – playwright and TV personality Henry Livings. There are also bands in Stalybridge and Greenfield.

Food, accommodation and shopping

The process of touristalization, described in the introduction, has just started in the towns along this route, which means there are not many guest houses yet, although a number of the pubs offer accommodation. The telephone exchanges to look for in the phone book are Mossley and Saddleworth (Manchester North Yellow Pages), and Huddersfield (Bradford Yellow Pages). There are a number of places to stay in Greenfield, but this is not very far along the route, while Uppermill offers bed and breakfast accommodation in houses and farmhouses. Near Delph (on the main A62 road) is the Cottage Hotel, an old farm high on the moors converted into a luxury hotel, with views that include the Roman fort.

For pub grub, the Waggon in Uppermill (which welcomes children and pushchairs in the lounge) and the Diggle both combine good food and good beer; but don't forget to check when food is available. High in the hills near Saddleworth Church is the Cross Keys with good food and drink, a playground for children and a room preserved in seventeenth century style which recently starred in an American television film on the origins of trade unions in Britain. The Diggle Hotel stands at a scenic spot on your route, and the Floating Light nearby on the main road. If you want to dance at the end of the day you will usually have to go to Stalybridge, Oldham or Huddersfield. There is a disco at the Railway at Marsden. This is also one of the pubs at which the Micron Theatre performs, see below. There are two health clubs in Uppermill and a sauna nearby in Shaw. Mossley, Uppermill and Marsden have craft centres.

Special events and places to visit

The Saddleworth Festival (late August) must be one of the most spectacular of British festivals – and all too little known. A colourful procession of morris dancers and others – including a man perched precariously on top of a cart piled with two and half tons of rushes – marches, wanders or staggers up and down hill for six miles across Saddleworth. The ceremony goes back to the days when rushes were used for floor coverings in Church. The procession takes place on the Saturday; it starts from Greenfield, goes through Uppermill and Dobcross, and ends at Delph, stopping at the pubs on the way. On the Sunday there is dancing and wrestling and other country sports on the fields around Saddleworth Church. Worth a trip from Paris, let alone London. Other features of Saddleworth include the Brass Band contests, which take place in many of the villages on Whit Friday, in late May or early July. Every four years there is a Festival of the Arts in Uppermill which attracts top class international talent. The next one as I write is May 1987. If that is over when you read this, you will have to wait until 1991. Bad luck, but this festival is only part of a musical tradition in the area; I once attended a spirited performance of a Handel opera in Saddleworth School. There are also art galleries in both Uppermill and Delph with paintings by local artists. A more recent initiative is a Roman chariot race around Uppermill in early October, and a children's 'pop' marathon the same weekend, both designed to raise money for charity. A variety of costumes appear in the chariot race, which is six and a half miles up and down hill; the teams take anything between one hour and three and a half to complete the course. Also in October is a race – the 'Autumn Leaves Half Marathon' – which is run over the hills and through the villages of Saddleworth.

The Huddersfield Canal Society organizes a canal festival at Ashton-under-Lyne in late July. This lasts a whole weekend and is set in an old canal basin, the meeting point of three canals with historic bridges and canal buildings designed with great attention to detail, their grey stone offsetting the colourful scene.

There is a rally of boats painted in the traditional reds and yellows and greens of the waterways with their floral and rural scenes; the landscapes in these paintings are dominated by castles. The designs are thought to have gipsy origin, while the castles represent the boatmen's dreams of riches. Some of the crews are dressed in the costumes of the nineteenth century boat people. In the arena there are stalls, side shows, brass bands, dancing and much else; boat trips are also on offer. There are other festivals in this valley of festivals and in Marsden on the other side of the Pennines as well. In Uppermill there is a museum of local history, which combines textile machinery with a gallery of local paintings. There is also a working mill which is open to the public. Near Marsden are the tunnel end cottages, once occupied by canal staff and now a visitor centre and a canal museum.

The route for the walkers

Remember to watch for the intentional mistake

At Stalybridge station exit turn sharp right and pass under the railway bridge. By looking backwards to the right after the bridge you can see one of the surviving views of a cotton landscape. The mills were mostly built around the turn of the century, of red brick with four storeys, as opposed to the earlier and smaller stone buildings you will see later. Each has its tower where originally the shafting from one mighty steam engine drove the machinery on all the floors. The most striking (the Queen mill) had a green dome, but has now disappeared. Walk straight along the road (Market Street) to the stone-built Town Hall (1882) (*6 minutes*). This is typical of the style of a northern town, although not as elaborate as some. Stalybridge, with its own local authority founded in 1828, used to be the capital of part of Cheshire until 1974. The ancient boundaries of Lancashire, Yorkshire, Cheshire and Derbyshire are all near this walk, and the river Tame was once an international frontier (between Northumbria and Mercia). Where the ancients fought over territory, their Victorian descendants rioted. Stalybridge is a peaceful town now, so little in the news that you have probably never heard of it, but urban violence was once a way of life there caused either by religion or hunger. As recently as 1868 Catholics and Protestants were slogging it out in the streets, and for 60 years before that food riots broke out when trade took a downturn. The 1860s were particularly hard times for the cotton industry; supplies to the mills were cut off during the war between the States in North America. In March 1863, for instance, the police could no longer cope and the army was called out. Aid for the unemployed workers came from collections held in American cities even during the most desperate period of their civil war. Some of the first modern-style factories in the world were built in this town, including a cotton-mill in 1776 which went over to steam twenty years later. Road improvements in the eighteenth century, and the building of the canal, brought transport to the town. Progress also brought its disasters – but, naturally – and in 1803 one of the canal reservoirs burst its banks causing great loss of life.

Don't get yourself run over as you hang avidly on these words and don't forget to turn right at the Town Hall; cross the river Tame by the Jubilee bridge, another piece of Victoriana like much of the town centre. Stalybridge is now in the Metropolitan Borough of Tameside. This part of the route can be followed on chart 1.

Pass the market on your left and then turn left into Corporation Street. At the other end of this street there was a pub (it's come down in the world since, being now a Conservative club) where the song 'It's a long way to Tipperary' was written. That was in 1913 and the author was so thrilled with it he ran across the road and sang it in the theatre (long since demolished). Since then rival armies have marched to many a skirmish singing 'My heart's right there'. You are walking in the opposite direction – eastwards – and on the right hand side is a Church with a churchyard which grows vegetables instead of gravestones, at least it did when this was written. Further on there is a public carpark on the right outside the old public baths *(3 minutes)*. Walk down the left hand side of the road to have a look at the river and turn right at the bridge into Mottram Road *(3 minutes)*. Look out for Lock Side on your left (just before a fork in the main road, at this point you turn left along the tow-path of the Huddersfield Narrow Canal *(3 minutes)*.

Note: this path is not suitable for pushchairs in wet weather; it is ideal for dogs as there are no sheep. The canal starts about two miles west at Ashton-under-Lyne where it is linked to the national system through the Ashton and High Peak canals which converge there (the site of the canal festival). But official vandalism some years ago led to culverting through much of Stalybridge. There are now ambitious plans to reopen the canal for boats by making part of the river Tame navigable and bypassing the culverted section. Yes, if you are thinking what I think you are, go back and have another look at the river. They mean it, however impossible it looks – a determined lot these Penniners, especially when they become canal fanatics. 'Grit' is the word. The towpath here is on the right hand side of the canal. Spare a minute to look back across the road at the old warehouses with their lifting-gear for loading the narrowboats. You will know that you are beside the canal by the notices. Obviously British Waterways are so overcome with admiration at themselves for allowing you to walk along the banks at all, that they have to prohibit anything they can think of. Do not swim, they say, probably for fear that you will blame them if you drown or catch typhoid. Do not ride horses or bicycles. There is no mention of motorbikes, probably they were not invented when British Waterways made the rules. With all the do nots, there is no mention of what you do, like getting a licence before you fish or launch your canoe. Do also remember that the path is private property and your ability to walk is not of right.

Walk along the canal and under two bridges. The one at an extraordinary angle carries the remains of a disused railway we shall meet again later, the other is a

Next door to Hartshead Pike stands a pub, which is also a farm, called the Colliers' Arms. You cannot see it from where you are standing now, but let me tell you about it. The grey stone buildings are squat, designed to withstand the worst sieges the weather can impose. The door was locked when I called, but the landlord opened and when asked whether the pub was open replied: 'I don't know.' After taking a few minutes to make up his mind he served me on condition that I drank outside so that he could lock up again. This must be normal, because I discovered that a long stretch of wall had been cemented over to make seats. The Colliers, after whose arms the pub is named, have long since disappeared with the closure of the mine; but there are still memories long enough to tell of the days when the men were paid in the pub – a practice long since made illegal because too much of the money went to the landlord rather than the miner's wife. The one room now doubles as a family sitting room and a pub lounge when the weather is too bad for sitting on the wall. If you want to go there, it is a mile and a half north of the A670 road just west of Mossley.

Turn back to the Castle Farm and begin the action again by looking diagonally right to a footpath sign *(3 minutes)*. Walk up to this and along the path which is also a bridleway, so you can cycle along it if you want to. The signpost says: 'Chew Valley, 2m.' indicating one of the livelier little rivers around here, a tributary of the Tame, which produces a fair torrent during the monsoon season (most of the year). This stretch is rough, but just possible for a pushchair except when very wet. All dogs should be on the lead as there are sheep in these parts. Look across the valley and share a piece of knowledge the Romans did not have by noticing the hollows in the hills ground out by the glaciers when the land was covered in ice. Rocks from the Lake District and even the south of Scotland were brought down here by those glaciers. The path you are on goes down and then up again - it would, wouldn't it? - *(12 minutes)*. Eventually it crosses a small stream where you can see a sharp bend on a road below you; at this point you keep to the main path which forks left *(5 minutes)*. The old cobbles survive here down to a house after which the surface is tarred up to a steep left bend where you cross yet another stream and walk up to a road junction. You have now arrived at Abraham's Chair *(6 minutes)*.

STOP, have a rest and take in the scenery. Look next at the houses on your right – the remains of an early industrial settlement. These settlements were built up the hillsides mainly to use the available water power and the cheap land. The site was also very remote which was convenient; it was out of sight of any wandering philanthropist who might question the working conditions of the children recruited from the city orphanages for long hours of work and early death. Spare a thought for the boys and girls who were tortured to death to make Britain rich; we shall meet one who survived in route seven.

Chart 3 shows the layout of paths at Abraham's chair.

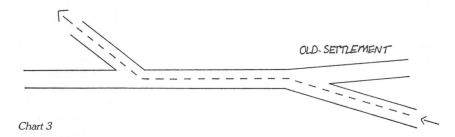

OLD-SETTLEMENT

Chart 3

You fork right when you start again, and follow the path up and down until you come to a junction with a footpath sign *(12 minutes)*. STOP again and look at the hills in front of you. They do not threaten you as they did our ancestors, you can escape to the pubs and cafes in the valley below; they can put you in your place, though, they are bigger than you. In front is a war memorial and some rocks known hereabouts as the Pots and Pans.

The Pots and Pans Rocks and the Saddleworth War Memorial.

Carry straight on after looking round, noting the rocky escarpment on the right. Follow the road downhill over yet another stream and through some S bends (where other roads join both from the left and from the right) until you reach the main road to Holmfirth, the A 635 *(7 minutes).* You will not be going there today but Holmfirth, high in the Pennines, is a town to see. It is a centre of the picture postcard industry and was once the unlikely setting for pioneer film-making. Now it has become famous again as the Summer Wine country. (For overseas visitors – 'The Last of the Summer Wine' is a popular television series). Spot the BBC types in the local pubs (no problem when they are in season).

At the road junction stands Scott's Mill (the Oak View Mills) and the beginnings of the town of Greenfield. Among the other mills nearby is the Royal George where the felt in your piano is likely to have been made; the firm supplies most of the big names in piano-making in Western Europe, Eastern Europe, America and now the Far East as well. Its mill pond is now a sanctuary for waterbirds.

Turn left and immediately right onto a rough track *(1 minute),* see chart 4. You might meet the carbound on an optional diversion; do not stop as there will be plenty of time to gossip later. After turning off the main road turn right and soon left, past a pond and between some small factories, and right again across the river by footbridge *(4 minutes).*

LAYOUT OF ROADS AND PATHS AT GREENFIELD

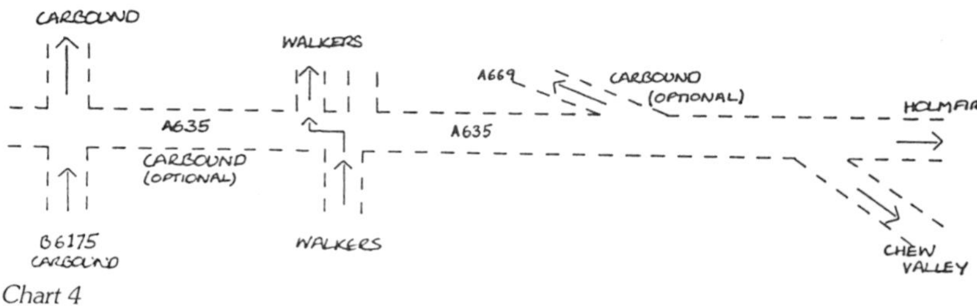

CARBOUND   WALKERS   A669   CARBOUND (OPTIONAL)   HOLMFIRTH

A635   A635

CARBOUND (OPTIONAL)

B6175 CARBOUND   WALKERS   CHEW VALLEY

Chart 4

Cross two roads and then another, called 'Higher Arthurs' – yes, that really is its name – and back on the route of the disused railway *(4 minutes).* Leave that on the right as you take the lower path and look out for a small letter box on your right *(2 minutes).* Opposite this, turn left down an unmarked track between some houses. Follow the path as it turns both right and left to a road and then turn right *(2 minutes).* By a pavilion turn left into Churchill field and keep left beside the river *(2 minutes).* The children can enjoy the 'Fun 'n Fitness' trail around this field. At the far left corner, leave the park, cross the main road and you are in Uppermill *(10 minutes).*
STOP and linger in Uppermill. Both the carbound and the walkers arrive at the

carpark which is at the start of the village (if full there is another to the right of the main road). Above you is the canal, dark in the trees here and alive with several sorts of duck; you can take a ride along the canal in a long boat. Beyond the carpark is a museum of local history, run by voluntary labour and full of the riches of the area including pictures by local artists. You can obtain leaflets here, at the public library along the main road or at the visitor centre along the canal.

The Huddersfield Narrow Canal beside Uppermill Museum.

After rest and refreshment find your way back to the canal. Walk among the mallards (the male has a green head, the female is speckled brown all over), the pochards (the male has a red head with a brown female) and the muscovies (larger ducks that have reverted to the wild, they have red in their black and white heads). The smaller black water-birds with the red bills and white stripes on the sides and rump are the moorhens. You move on to chart 5 here.

The path is under the trees on the far side of the canal, but crosses at the first bridge *(3 minutes)*. The tow path had to change sides from time to time to make life easier for the horses. Walk along a bank with the canal on one side and the river Tame, wide and shallow and with stepping stones at this point, on the right *(1 minute)*. At the next lock the railway viaduct comes into view, the much repaired stones striding across the landscape *(4 minutes)*. On the far side of the valley is another of the derelict railways of these parts, the scenic branch line to Delph – the Delph donkey as it was called because the company that built it used horses when they could not afford engines *(3 minutes)*. The track provides another walk if you have time. Meanwhile right underneath the viaduct is the next lock, built on an aqueduct with the river far below and now restored to use.

STOP. You are still in the valley with its wooded scenery and you are surrounded and overshadowed by the works of man. The viaduct was sculpted by stone masons long since dead, many of them no doubt killed by the deadly dust – bed-bound, choking and spitting blood for the last few years of their lives, nature's reward for their skill and hard work. Think of them here and at every lock and bridge, and marvel at the surfeit of skill which they lavished on the bridges, the viaducts and the carefully designed approaches to the locks. Behind you is a visitor centre, not to be missed for its fascinating and ever-changing exhibitions.

On one of the bridges near this lock you can see the grooves in the stone due to wear from the ropes attached to the horses, but before you march on there is something else to look at. On the far side of the lock there is a curious-looking fixture, a small metal cylinder with some holes in it. Try offering each of your companions three guesses as to what that's for, with a forfeit for a wrong answer. Better not make it a ducking in the canal in case there is an official of British Waterways watching. The river would be less illegal. The answer: to pull the plug out. Get your breath back and read on. If the canal needed repair, part could be sealed off by specially shaped boards. In each section there was a plug in the bottom of the canal which would allow it to be drained. This plug was in the lock and emptied it into the river below. A chain was attached to the cylinder and to the plug. Then a lever was also inserted into the cylinder and – heave – out came the plug. Some years ago, on another waterway, a dredger accidentally pulled a plug out and found itself on dry land. In the walls of the lock you can make out the marks of the stone masons who built it.

Walk on quickly to get dry after your ducking and find where the canal widens at the place the barges used to turn. This was also a junction with a branch canal which went to a mill on the right *(3 minutes)*. You can find the remains of the now filled in branch if you search. On the far bank you will see the Wool Road Warehouse. The building, which has been restored, stands at the original terminus of the canal. Picture the narrow boats arriving and the queue of packhorses (600 for each boat) waiting to take the goods on the next stage of their journey over the Pennines to the boats on the waterways the other side. You may like to discuss how the horses and the boats ever managed to arrive at the right place at the right time. Nowadays with the telephones, telexes, on line links and the rest chaos can arise over easier problems than that, so how did they manage?

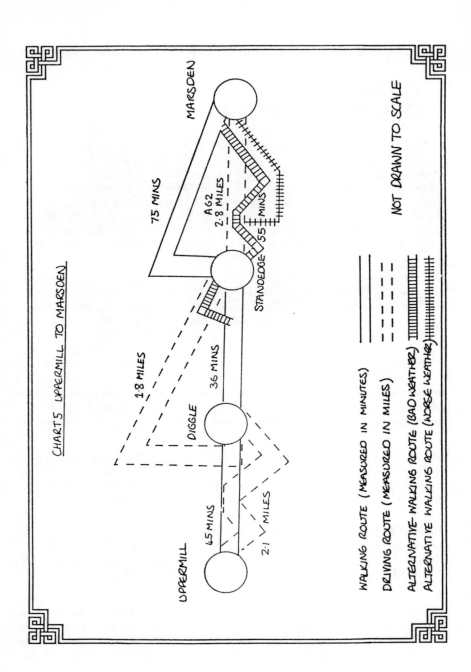

CHART 5 UPPERMILL TO MARSDEN

MARSDEN

75 MINS

A62
2·8 MILES

STANDEDGE 55 MINS

1·8 MILES

36 MINS

DIGGLE

45 MINS

UPPERMILL

2·1 MILES

WALKING ROUTE (MEASURED IN MINUTES)
DRIVING ROUTE (MEASURED IN MILES)
ALTERNATIVE WALKING ROUTE (BAD WEATHER)
ALTERNATIVE WALKING ROUTE (WORSE WEATHER)

NOT DRAWN TO SCALE

The canal and the railway.

Behind the warehouse is a mill which weaves plaids and which is open to the public. Here is a chance to see a mill in action; refreshments are available too. Part of the mill building is used to put together vintage cars, a sign of the times.

Beyond the warehouse, the canal is culverted under the road (I hope this information will soon be out-of-date) and you have to detect a narrow entrance between the houses across the road *(1 minute)*. There is also a bus stop here from which you can go back if you are overcome by your efforts so far.

The next lock is the first of a series climbing up the hillside *(2 minutes)*. The scenery is changing; the wooded valley gives way to the grassy hills, the willowherb to the heather. Another chance of a guessing competition is provided by the width of the passages between the locks. Why are they so wide?

If you guessed, like I did, that the answer is to make space for the queues of boats waiting to go through, you guessed wrong and the forfeit this time is to kiss the feet of the next hiker you meet. The queues would form at the top and bottom, not between the locks. Obvious? The correct answer, it appears, is to store water to replace that lost through the lock gates below. Water can drain away fast when a canal is climbing so rapidly.

Wool Road: the original warehouse.

Proceed, with the railway on your right and a typical mill scene on your left. You follow the tow-path past five locks and come eventually to a flat stretch *(12 minutes)*. Across the water is the wharf of the Shaw Mill which now makes pallets. You will have noticed the proprietor's house, a relic of the days when the boss lived on the job. The house has a clocktower to make sure the workers had no excuse for being late for work. This reminds me of a similar clocktower in another part of the country where two of the faces have been removed. The removal was ordered by the landowner who decided that his workers were spending too much of their working day watching the clock. He left the faces that could be seen from their homes.

Beyond the factory (and close to a footbridge over the railway) is a pedestrian subway of two centuries ago. Go through this dark, damp passage under the canal. They built nobbly walls in those days, not plastic surfaces designed for graffiti-mongers like the moderns. Imagine the weary trek home from work through the tunnel on a dark winter evening with only a shawl and clogs to protect you from the cold *(3 minutes)*.

By the next lock the rounded head of the valley is beginning to close in upon you, and the human settlements are scattered among the grass and rocks, white or black against the green *(3 minutes)*. Rub your fingers along one of the walls *(after you have eaten your sandwiches)* to uncover the dirt of industrialization.

The next lock is the last on the way up *(3 minutes)*. You are now 42 locks away from where the canal starts in Ashton-under-Lyne, 60 locks from Manchester, and 656 feet above sea level. Worth Mill, which has lost its chimneys, is passed on the left and a level stretch brings you to the mouth of Standedge Tunnel *(6 minutes)*.

Standedge: the canal enters a 3-mile tunnel.

Do not be misled when you see 1893 over the entrance, that was the date when the tunnel was moved. Yes, moved – to make room for more railway expansion. The opening of this civil engineering landmark was in 1811; it took 16 years to build – the estimate was for 5 years, how times have not changed. This is the longest canal tunnel and the highest stretch of canal in the country.

The tunnel looks down at heel now, but there are hopes of reopening it as a tourist attraction. The tourists will go through in electrically propelled boats, the canal boats were pushed by men called leggers lying on their backs walking their legs along the rock – for over three miles. The tunnel had no towpath, so the boatmen walked the horses over the mountain to meet their boat the other side while the full-time leggers pushed it through. After examining your back and legs and deciding how they would stand up to legging for three miles, walk into Diggle and onto the road. You pass the bus stop and turn right onto the railway bridge. The station no longer exists, but in front of you are three rail tunnels, all built at different times. All have access to the canal along which the earth and rock was brought out during the rail tunnel building. The canal was slightly rerouted and the two earlier tunnels closed when the newest one was built in the 1890s. The locals tell me that the disused rail tunnels have been much explored, but you will not want to chance a public flogging, or whatever they award these days for trespassing on railway company property, and will prefer to cross the bridge and find food and drink at the Diggle Hotel *(1 minute)*. You can sit in the garden on the day in the year when the weather permits; this is yet another place with a bus service if you want to chicken out.

The path continues on the left hand side of the pub, the way the horses went. As you climb, look out on your right and note an early industrial settlement, black against the dark green. That's the Diggle Mill, another of those places where the prosperity of Britain was well and truly laid. You might see a haunted mill further up where the moaning and the weeping of the child slaves can still be heard, they tell me. In a cottage in these hills a badly wounded soldier was once cured by an old lady who covered his wounds with the mould from the top of a jam jar. That was in 1745 after a skirmish during the Jacobite rebellion.

Keep on walking, the track swings left after passing some buildings on the right. Then, beside a restored farmhouse called Far Diggle Edge, STOP *(18 minutes)*. You can look down the valley, over the tunnel ventilator, and see just how the Pennines absorb the efforts of man and survive.

Walk on a few yards and then turn sharp right up a narrow path between broken walls. Watch your legs, this path is treacherous; do not use it if there is ice or snow; but carry straight on until you come to a minor road which climbs steeply to join the A 62 near the top. This is the first bad weather stretch shown on Chart 5.

After climbing up between the two walls, follow the one on the left when they part; soon you cross a stream *(8 minutes)*. Continue along the wall, you will see a spoil tip behind it, and turn left when another path crosses *(2 minutes)*. There is now a tunnel ventilator, another one, on your left and a house on your right *(3 minutes)*. When the path crosses a small stream, you can see the remains of an old bridge and a gate with access to the reservoir above you. At this point fork right and along a small path which takes you up the side of the dam after crossing a small stone bridge. At the corner of the reservoir, join the A 62 (together with the bad weather route and the carbound), and walk along the reservoir to the carpark *(5 minutes)*. You are now at Standedge, the Pennine watershed, 1,270 feet above the sea; the main road goes straight ahead through a cutting. You are also at the modern county boundary of Greater Manchester and West Yorkshire. There is usually a caravan selling refreshments in the carpark.

You now have several choices according to the weather and your condition. You can:

Go on. You have three routes to choose from.

Go back. Either by following the route you came up or by following the minor road which turns left off the main road just beyond the reservoir and takes you back to Diggle, or by circling back to Uppermill via Delph.

To go by Delph, you cross the main road and walk about 100 yards along the Pennine Way northwards until you come to a left fork. Follow the path down past some houses to a road; go along the road for a few yards and then fork left on a bridle way over a hill. Where two rough roads cross turn right. This brings you into Delph. Follow the main road down to the crossroads and turn left, passing the remains of Delph station on your right; a short distance along the road and on the right is an entry to the track that follows the path of the disused railway. This will bring you back to Uppermill.

Give up for today. In this case you can either wait for a bus, thumb a lift or walk to the nearest pub; there is one a few minutes' walk both ways along the main road. There is also accommodation within half a mile in each direction.

If you decide to go on, take a look at the weather. The route I recommend is not suitable in ice or snow and can be deadly in mist. So I give two other options.

In fine weather, cross the road and follow the wide track which starts opposite the carpark. This is part of the Pennine Way. Turn off almost immediately at a right fork *(7 minutes)*. A wide path is followed until an overgrown track crosses. At this point use your compass and strike across country going due north. You have a short period of rough walking up and down on peat bogs when the more distant views disappear. After a while you can see the Redbrook Reservoir on the right; this is the home of a sailing club and is usually colourful with dinghies at the weekend. It was built for the canal which it supplies through a vertical shaft down to the tunnel, 300 feet below. When you reach the highest point you have a view of the Colne valley to the east of the Pennines; you pick up a track after crossing a stream.

By now your route is swinging round to the east and you can see trees and houses and the main road below. Pass the first valley and follow the second which takes you steeply down to the right and onto a path again, after some rough walking, which leads to the junction of two valleys marked by a water inspection cover *(30 minutes)*. These moors are inhabited by a number of birds for most of the year – grouse, plovers, curlews, skylarks and crows. Look out for the red grouse, a large reddish-brown bird which flies out of the peat mounds with a fussy squawk. Watch also for the two kinds of plover. The lapwing, which most people know by sight, has a crest on the back of its head, rounded wings, is black and white and cries pee-weet (two syllables). The golden plover has pointed wings, black and gold upper parts and a single-syllable cry. Both plovers desert the high moors in winter.

The path continues eastward and downwards to a stone bridge (seventeenth century), called Eastergate because the villagers once walked in procession round here at Easter *(5 minutes)*. This is another haunted place; a man who was thrown off his horse and drowned in a flood lurks around the bridge which you now cross. Turn right along the river bank. Right again when you reach the small road. There used to be a brewery up to the left, and a short way along the road there was also a mill on the left *(5 minutes)*. The house is now a hotel and the millpond has become a trout pool. The route has descended into a wooded valley, a contrast to the open moorland, and soon passes the old brewery stables, now cottages and beautifully converted; there is no need to tell the occupants how well-kept they are, every other passer by will have done that. Follow the road to the Junction pub, fork right and down to the canal *(20 minutes)*. Stand on the bridge and stop, you will need to by now, and look at the tunnel entrance. Here, as along other canals and rivers, you may see parties of small yellow and green birds in winter. These are not canaries but siskins which move restlessly about and settle on the alder shrubs which are common around here.

If the weather is too bad for the moorland route just described, do not cross the road at the summit of the Standedge pass, but scramble up a footpath on the far side of the carpark that is signposted for the Pennine Way, southbound. This is the route marked 'alternative walking route (bad weather)' on chart 5. It is the route for pushchairs in *good weather,* although you may have to carry them in places. If you have scrambled up the bank, fork left in about 1-200 yards when the Pennine Way path swings round to the right. This path leads back to the road which it rejoins beside the Redbrook sailing club and opposite the Great Western Hotel. Keep on the right hand side of the road junction *(5 minutes)*.

The minor road turning right at this junction is marked on the chart as 'Alternative walking route (worse weather)' and leads down into Marsden. At the fork both roads lead to the same place, but the left hand one is a little shorter and a little steeper. If not following this keep along the main road a little further, passing the Eagle's Nest on the right *(3 minutes)*. Beyond this pub are two paths climbing up to the right *(5 minutes)*. Take the second which passes a derelict building and two tunnel ventilators to come to the top of the hill where another path joins from the right *(12 minutes)*. Walk on to the next ventilator from which there is a wide view of the Colne Valley with hill settlements to be seen in all directions *(10 minutes)*.

Walk steeply down the hillside to the left of the ventilator to pick up a path which swings right past a few houses and then turns sharp left between the houses to join a track *(10 minutes)*. When this joins the main road, turn right and almost immediately left down a winding lane *(5 minutes)*. When you come to a small reservoir on the left, find a path on the right which leads down to the canal. Walk to the bridge and rejoin the fine weather route *(5 minutes)*.

On one side can be seen the entrance to the tunnel which has brought the canal from Diggle and the three railway tunnels. In the foreground stand two canal cottages both recently restored. They are now joined together and house a visitor centre and an exhibition about the Huddersfield Canal. You can get refreshments here. In the other direction from the bridge, you face the local depot of the British Waterways Board. This part of the canal has been restored while this book was being written. You now follow the towpath through the rich foliage to the first lock. On the left is the canal with the railway station beyond, on the right is the Railway Inn with good beer, food and a disco *(5 minutes)*.

This is one of the canalside pubs where you can see the Micron theatre, an experience not to be missed. This small company performs all over the country, usually in canal side pubs. Their permanent home is a narrowboat which settles near here for the winter. Do support them – the Arts Council, which is supposed to be making the arts more widely available, has withdrawn support from a company which is doing just that. They visit Marsden in mid-September at the time of the Marsden Festival, so plan on being here at that time of year; if that is impossible, they tour most of the canal system.

Among its other claims to fame, Marsden is the town in which General Wolfe's mother was born – her son captured Quebec.

Marsden is also the end of this route, so once again you have some stopping and deciding to do. You can:

Stop here. There are bed and breakfast places and several hotels in the neighbourhood.

Go back. The trains are few on weekdays, even less on Saturdays and non-existent on Sundays. The buses are also infrequent, so check before you start. You can walk back by the rough weather route which is shorter and brings you to Standedge quickly enough.

Go on. You can walk along the canal to Huddersfield, about 7 miles, or go by train or bus; both are more frequent in that direction.

The route for the carbound

From Stalybridge station start along Market Street. This is a one-way street so you will need to turn left and then right to arrive at the same point as the walkers.

Follow walking route until Lock Side on Mottram Road. Stop and look at the canal then continue along the road which forks left, the B6175.

Follow the B6175 (see chart 1) as it undulates along; if you look carefully you can see the ruins of Staly Hall (the seat of the family which gave Stalybridge its name) between the houses on the left before you zigzag into the village of Millbrook. Note a classic mill village, also on your left, best seen before the zig and the restored cottages seen to advantage after the zag. One of the mills here was originally built to make chains for slaves; another example of a trade which made the country rich. Console yourself for having to drive, by noting the view across the valley. Note on your right the Roman Catholic Church which brings a flavour, not to mention a colour, of Italy into the blacks and greens of the hills. Soon you will see the Buckton Castle Inn on your left.

The carbound have to wait here to let the walkers catch up. When you reach the Buckton Castle Inn, you can turn left down Lowswood Road and then right onto the dirt track to meet the walkers. You can even drive, if you have a light vehicle, to the mouth of Scout Tunnel for a glimpse of the canal. Turn back and, for a short time, follow the same route as the walkers.

Walkers and carbound now move on to chart 2; the carbound keep straight ahead when the walkers turn onto a bridleway and turn right when rejoining the B6175, moving on to chart 2.

The remains of Staly Hall.

Soon you will cross the A635 near to the path the walkers are following (see chart 4). If you have some time to spare, you might like to turn right at these crossroads (if you are at the right place the Royal George Inn is on your left – the nearby Royal George Mill makes piano felt and exports it to the piano manufacturers of the world). If you do turn right, you drive up into the Chew Valley, which you will see in about a mile on your right. There's a reservoir at the bottom used by a sailing club. You won't be able to see the top, but the hills here are very rocky. The reason is because two giants on top of these hills fought a battle for the love of a beautiful shepherdess; while she lay naked on the hillside, they were slinging huge rocks at one another. When her favourite was killed, she threw herself over a precipice. Aah!

You can now either go on and have a quick look at Holmfirth (the 'Summer Wine' country) or turn back. In either case you can turn right in Greenfield and follow the A669 to Greenfield station, turning right onto the A670m for Uppermill.

If you do not take the diversion, you keep on the B6175 which also brings you to Greenfield station, the A670 and Uppermill. The carbound can meet the walkers here; if they do not have any to meet, they will drive through Uppermill and continue a short distance until they come to the railway viaduct. Stop and look at the visitor centre, then turn back sharp to the right and up a steep hill).

Follow the road round to the left and then sharp right (by a stable, a bridle path goes straight on) and then at the top of a hill where four roads join keep left and look out for a right turn down another steep hill. This brings you down to Diggle and the Diggle Hotel. The walkers will approach from the other side of the railway bridge.

After leaving the Hotel the carbound will cross the path of the walkers by going over the railway bridge. After a short distance they come to a T-junction where they turn right and drive up a steep hill, eventually joining the A62 just before the top and meeting up with the walkers again at the carpark at Standedge.

After the top of the hill the carbound turn right (following the 'alternative walking route (worse weather)' on chart 5). On the left, at the bottom of the hill, there is a millpond with toilets nearby. You then drive under the main road past the Church, which you may like to look at; the river is also picturesque just here. The road then swings round to the right beside the Railway Inn, and on over the canal and the railway, keeping left. When you come to another pub, The Junction, on your right, you turn sharp back left and reach the tunnel end cottages described in the walking route.

You can either stay around here or go back to base; but if you are driving on to Littleborough (route 4), you need only go back to the visitor centre before Uppermill, and turn right for Delph (see below).

Links to next route

By public transport: Return to Manchester and then train to Littleborough.

By car: from Stalybridge, turn left for Delph (A6052) after Uppermill. At Junction, across crossroads and onto the A640. This brings you over the hills, past the Moorcock Restaurant, and under the motorway and into Milnrow. At the traffic lights turn right and immediately left, up a hill and left again (signposts: Littleborough or Hollingworth Lake); after about two miles, right at T junction, follow the road round past the lake and turn left on arriving at Littleborough **by**

By walking: Follow the route of the old railway from Uppermill to Delph, then footpath to Denshaw (part minor roads), cross A640 and footpaths via Piethorn reservoir, going under the M62 at Rakethorn and past Hollingworth Lake into Littleborough.

Booklets on Saddleworth

This area has a number of societies producing excellent booklets, including:

The Saddleworth Civic Trust. A series of booklets on the area.

The Saddleworth Historical Society. A series of leaflets entitled 'Local History Trails.'

The Huddersfield Canal Society. A leaflet entitled 'A Unique Waterway' and other papers on the canal.

In addition there are two maps of the area with descriptions entitled 'Saddleworth, Countryside Guide,' published 'by a committee or representatives from local societies.'

Oldham Borough Council have published an illustrated booklet called 'Saddleworth Visitor Guide'.

A booklet I enjoyed especially was *Saddleworth Seven One Two*, an account of the building of the Roman roads in these parts, edited by Donald Haigh and published by Bradford Grammar School.

Route 4

Littleborough and Summit

Maps to use for this route: Ordnance Survey Leisure Series (1:25,000) 'The South Pennines'. The 1:50,000 series is a problem—you need three (nos. 109, 110 and 103 although most of the walk is on 109 'Manchester'. The grid reference for Littleborough station is 938163.

Littleborough is the centre for route 4. Ever heard of it? Perhaps you have, but a lot of people have not and that's one of its advantages. It stands on a busy main road, but you can soon get away from the noise. There is a wide square to the south of the main road where the bus and railway stations are. Littleborough has two information centres. One is a heritage centre in a former hotel stable building (on Lodge St. tel: 0706 78481), easy to find, two minutes walk across that main road from the town centre. Here you will receive a warm welcome as well as information about the area. The other we will come to later. The town centre contains a pub (the Wheatsheaf, built in 1792) with an extraordinary outside, it looks like a mini-castle and is obviously interesting if you are keen on architecture. The inside is even more extraordinary—a century of bric-a-brac; a few minutes' walk away, also across that main road, is the parish church with its perpendicular windows. Between the two is one of the best second-hand bookshops in Greater Manchester—another hobby to add to the growing list. You can also add water-skiing. Romans, Danes and Vikings invaded this area in the past.

Food, accommodation and shopping

The exchanges to look for under hotels or restaurants in the yellow pages are Littleborough and Ripponden. there are numerous bed and breakfast places and some small hotels.

The area has three fine restaurants. One is the Moorcock. Be sure to get the right one, this is a common name round here. The restaurant is at Denshaw on the road over from Saddleworth (route 3) and is about six miles south of Littleborough (B6225 to Milnrow and then A640—sorry you need a car or taxi for this one). There is Over the Bridge at Ripponden (see carbound route); and overlooking Hollingworth Lake is an Italian restaurant—Ristorante del Largo—

which offers especially good value as well as a warm welcome. On Sundays lunch is served all the afternoon.

There is a trout farm where you can buy fresh fish in the hills above Littleborough (see carbound route).

How to get there

You can come by train – there is an hourly service from Manchester, Bradford or Leeds – so it is easy to reach from anywhere in the country, but if you come from the south you will have to change stations at Manchester.

Littleborough station is something special. It is an example of the chunky stone architecture of the Pennine railways – we shall come across some even better examples in routes 5 and 6. It was also one of the early lines. There is a plaque on the station to say that George Stephenson – designer of pioneer locomotives like the Rocket – was present at the opening in 1839. For a couple of years, while Summit tunnel was being built, Littleborough was the terminus. It became the terminus again in 1984 when the tunnel was blown up, but we'll encounter that later.

You can also come here by bus. There are regular services from Manchester, Rochdale and Halifax.

If you come by car, Littleborough stands on the A58 from Rochdale to Halifax. It is also close to the M62. Turn off at exit 21 (Milnrow) north at the roundabout (left if you are travelling east!) and right at the first traffic lights; almost immediately turn left and up a steep hill and left again (before Gallows pub). Both these left turns signpost 'Hollingworth Lake.' Then right at T junction after about a mile. The road now bends left and passes Hollingworth Lake on your right, bending left again for the descent into Littleborough. When you join the main road turn left, and then left again after traffic lights. This brings you to the station. There is a car park along Peel Street, which leaves the centre on the left of the Wheatsheaf and right of the station.

In case you are confused by the directions around Littleborough, here is a chart of the town centre.

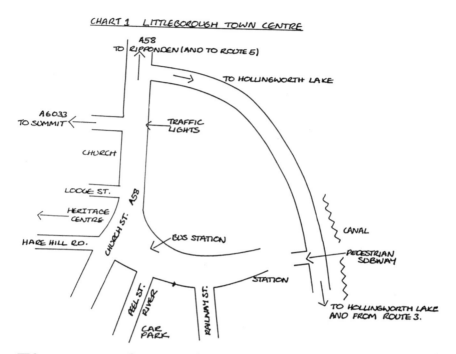

CHART 1 LITTLEBOROUGH TOWN CENTRE

A58
TO RIPPONDEN (AND TO ROUTE 5)

TO HOLLINGWORTH LAKE

A6033
TO SUMMIT

TRAFFIC
LIGHTS

CHURCH

LODGE ST.

CHURCH ST. A58

HERITAGE
CENTRE

CANAL

HARE HILL RD.

BUS STATION

PEDESTRIAN
SUBWAY

PEEL ST.

RIVER

RAILWAY ST.

STATION

TO HOLLINGWORTH LAKE
AND FROM ROUTE 3.

CAR
PARK

The route for walkers

Don't forget there is one deliberate mistake, see the quiz at the end of the book.

This route is ideal for all comers, from the pushchair stage to the hardiest long-distance walkers. I will give turning off points for those who do not want to go too far, and there is advice for the disabled. For the walkers, the route has been chosen from many possibilities to give the greatest variety. The part from the visitor centre to the White House is perfect in reasonable weather, but is hard going over peat when really wet and is dangerous in fog or snow. If the weather is too bad, you could short cut the first part by taking a Halifax bus from Littleborough to the Roman Road (only a few minutes). Walk up there and join the route on the Roman Road, turn left at the watercourse. The rest is clear and safe in all weathers.

If you are walking the whole route, you can make a luxury walk of this one and have a change from carrying sandwiches (although, I need hardly warn you, always carry some emergency rations). One of the times I walked this route, I left Littleborough at a quarter to eleven, had a cup of tea and a snack at the visitor centre (the refreshment bar does not open until 11.0), lunch at the White House soon after half past one and was back at Littleborough for five.

Start from Littleborough town centre (there are toilets here as well as train and bus stops). Go under the railway by the pedestrian subway, cross road and turn left along canal towpath. This is the Rochdale canal, a broad canal – meaning, as you will see, that the locks are broader than those of the Huddersfield you visited on the last route. This canal is also being restored and you will come across an example just *5 minutes* from your starting point when you turn a corner to find a reconstructed canal scene – a renovated lock, with all the trimmings, and a well-restored lock-keeper's house. Turn right over the bridge, across the lock and follow the path left and right. After this manoeuvre you can see a small chemical plant on your right and some houses on your left; the inhabitants hang out their washing across the street, so don't park your car there. Once past the houses, there's a high bank on the left which is the dam of a mill pond; do scramble up and have a look.

In less than *5 minutes* from the lock, you reach a 'private road' sign; but don't be put off – that is strictly for the cars. You follow past some well kept cottages and into a narrow valley, rich in flowers at the right time of year. After another 5 *minutes,* the path divides. Both hikers and those with young families keep to the main path which swings to the right and crosses two stiles.

Those with pushchairs, or otherwise wanting a more leisurely day of it, can come this far. The pushchairs may need a lift over the stiles but it should not take them more than another *5 minutes* to get to the Hollingworth Lake visitor centre.

I like this centre, outside as well as in. It is a modern building which yet fits neatly into the scene as if it had always been there. Inside there are all sorts of fascinating details about the area – its wildlife and its history. Did you know, for instance, that Captain Webb – the first man to swim the Channel – trained in Hollingworth Lake? He only lived 39 years because, after swimming the Channel, he became too ambitious and attempted Niagara – with tragic results.

The Visitor Centre, Hollingworth Lake.

The centre has refreshments, a bookstall, an imaginative exhibition showing the main features of the area – including the history and the natural history – together with helpful staff and *clean* toilets (some of the toilets on this route and the next are a disgrace to whoever is responsible). After refreshment you can walk round the lake. You could do it in half an hour, but allow double that because there are two children's playgrounds on the way round. Then return the way you came or, if you came by bus from Rochdale or Manchester, you can get a bus back from here.

Hollingworth Lake was built as a supply reservoir for the Rochdale canal, and had a pumping system to take water to those parts of the canal that gravity could not reach. The lake, well enough used these days, was once a major resort – before the locals could afford a trip to the seaside, which was before they could afford a trip to the Costa Brava. You can read the story – of Hollingworth Lake, that is, not of the Costa Brava – in one of the booklets recommended at the end of this chapter.

Hollingworth Lake.

The only blot on the horizon is the nearby viaduct of the M62. I am not taking you too near that, it is noisy and is crossed by a footbridge on the Pennine Way which must have been designed by a sadistic anti-hiker – it is a pain to cross as the wind whistles up the cutting and the lorries roar below. As I write another section of the Rochdale canal is under threat from the Department of Transport – that archaic institution which appears to exist for the purpose of transferring money from the pockets of the taxpayer to those of the road haulage companies – I hope the threat will have disappeared by the time you read this.

The hikers leave the visitor centre and turn left at the road. After *4 minutes,* fork left up a bridlepath and in another *4 minutes* there is a house on your left called 'Hollingworth Fold' with a camping ground. You are climbing steadily and in another *5 minutes* pass old mine workings and a spoil tip on your left and a restored house on your right. Note the warm brown stone, and the square windows offsetting the arch of the one-time stables. You are in a sheltered spot now; soon you will be on the open moor, struggling through soggy peat. Be prepared to turn back if the weather is too wet or foggy.

You are now walking steeply up a track in a narrow sheltered valley. When you come above the spoil tip, in about *8 minutes,* the signposted track swings to the right. Here, turn left and follow a grassy path up a slope with pylons on your right. Be prepared for an icy blast as you come out of the shelter of the valley, be prepared also for a ghostly roar from behind you. That comes from the traffic on the M62 – not far away but out of sight. If, by any mischance, you do wander into fog, the noise can help – it comes from due south of you. The M62 has its uses! It has to be admitted, also, that Littleborough would be swamped with traffic without the motorway which has also made the area more accessible. The Department of Transport also has its uses!

5 minutes later, cross another track, just below an electricity pylon, and continue upwards, following the path as it swings right and then left. In another *10 minutes* you pass a pond on your left. An isolated little natural water, this relic of the ice age reflects all the moods of the hills. The waters are deep and dark, with the surrounding grass reflected on the edge. If you are artistic you will want to stop and stare; if you are scientific, you will certainly explore the flora and fauna around the pond. If you are both – you can forget the idea of getting to the White House for lunch and eat your emergency rations.

Talking about fauna, there are plenty of whitened bones near the path. I presume these are from sheep that just failed to make it down the mountain when a blizzard set in. Take warning, these sheep are much tougher than you.

For another *25 minutes* the path is leading you steadily, and sometimes steeply, to the top of a hill (about 1400 feet). Near the end are some cairns at the last of which the path suddenly disappears. Worry not, but keep straight ahead, cursing the peat if it is wet, walking eastwards and then swinging north towards a rock formation now clearly visible on your left. Aim for a rock that appears to be precariously balanced on another at the beginning of the formation. In dry weather, you should reach this from the cairn in *15 minutes,* but it will take much longer when the peat is wet. Although this seems a bleak, high spot, there is much wild life. I have even seen wasps up here.

You now join the Pennine Way which is clearly marked most of the time; if in doubt keep along the rocks in a northerly direction, do not wander to the east. These rocks are called Blackstone Edge.

In another *20 minutes,* or more if the peat is very soft, you come to a fence with a gate; just beyond is a single standing stone called the Aigin Stone. This ancient landmark (Aigin probably means edging, a boundary mark or signpost) stands near the top of a steep track, the Roman Road. Turn left and walk down. As you go, you can see some of the lay-out of the track with a channel of carved stone in the middle. No one knows the origin of this. Some say it was made to fit the chariot wheels of the Romans, or their enemies, but most think it to be considerably more modern. One suggestion is that it was in the middle of the road and provided a primitive braking system on this steep slope. The carts going down would be dragging a heavy weight in the channel. To me it looks more like a drainage system, to prevent storm waters washing the road away.

Whatever its origin, this channel has been there a long time. Excavations are now going on to try to find the origins of the road.

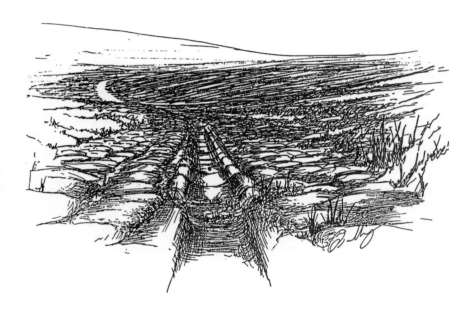

The Roman Road, looking down.

A famous traveller in these parts was Daniel Defoe, the author of Robinson Crusoe. He wrote about Blackstone Edge in one of his books – A Tour Through England and Wales, written two and a half centuries ago in 1724. He claims to have got lost in a blizzard, in *August,* and nearly fallen over a precipice. In 1724 they also had unusual weather, it seems. Incidentally he was full of praise for the people of these parts. The people of Rochdale he found most helpful ('the honest Rochdalemen' he called them); but his greatest praise was for Halifax where, he said, everyone was earning their own living from the age of four. No scruples about child labour, and that by one who was once prosecuted for his progressive opinions.

5 minutes after you start walking down the Roman Road you come to a point where a watercourse crosses. Turn right and follow the path beside this watercourse. After about *10 minutes,* you see a sediment trap (on the left of the path) in this old waterworks system – where some of the sediment in the water was extracted. Just beyond this is a disused quarry on the right. This is a magic place, go visit it and rest a few moments breathing in the atmosphere of a work of man thoroughly overcome by nature; here many shades of green and brown are mixed with great subtlety.

Getting hungry? Walk up to the gate which faces you, do not go through but turn sharp left and go steeply down to a road. Turn right and in *5 minutes* you will reach the White House (be careful how you cross the road, some lunatics race over the brow of the hill above you). I can thoroughly recommend the food, the drink and the service at the White House; there are also fine carpets, so leave your ruck-sack and boots outside. Make your way to the back room where there is a great view up the valley towards Summit. The reservoir below you is the Upper Chelburn and is used for water skiing. The hill on the far side of it is called Snoddle Hill (not many people know that!).

You leave the White House and walk up the road for a short distance, turning left at the Pennine Way sign and following the path beside the Blackstone Edge Reservoir. I have seen a group of wader birds called dunlins playing on the sand at the other end of this reservoir. They are smallish brown birds with long legs and long beaks more often seen at the seaside. Larger birds, but similar in appearance, are the curlews which swoop overhead and sometimes alight on the dry stone walls. The cry of the curlew is one of the distinctive sounds of the moors.

Curlew: the bird of the moors.

85

After about half an hour, go straight on when the path goes under some electric cables and keep on as it turns right and left. Walk along the side of the next reservoir, called Light Hazzles, and amuse yourselves trying to guess how it came by a name which is also used of the nearby hills.

At the beginning of the next reservoir, the Warland *(8 minutes),* fork left away from the reservoir and follow a track down to a corner of the reservoir. After *3 minutes* you will notice, close to your right, the elaborate design of the entry to the reservoir system; at a much greater distance on your left is a sensational view of the hills folding into one another. The track now turns left and you are walking parallel to a stream into a valley below.

In *5 minutes* you move from the dark green moorland to light green cultivated fields, walls and buildings. Continue down hill through two gates past a farm and a water authority building and on to a road (another *5 minutes).* Continue down through another gate *(8 minutes)* with a waterfall on the left and a variety of trees. Still downhill, follow the road past some restored houses as it winds through a wood and into an open valley. Here you reach the tow-path of the Rochdale canal, at a recently restored lock *(10 minutes).* A notice says that this restoration has had the support of the European Community. So that was the point of joining.

We are going to turn left, back to Littleborough, where we should arrive in *an hour and a quarter.* If you have a little while to spare, do turn right and walk a little way along the canal, round a bend. On the other side of the valley, and high in the hills, you can then see an old stone house. This is 'Rough Stones', the house in which the engineer lived while building the Summit tunnel which is running parallel to the canal and almost underneath that house. This tunnel was one of the first major railway tunnels ever built; it is over a mile long and was completed with great loss of life. Three men and two boys were killed in just one day in 1839. The tunnel was opened two years later and 143 years after that it was nearly destroyed, fortunately without loss of life. Many of you will have seen pictures of the flames coming out of one of the tunnel ventilators, and heard how the crew of the freight train heroically uncoupled the locomotive to salvage as much as they could. The ventilator is also just across the valley. Brick work melted, but the bricks were so thick that the tunnel survived and the railway reopened the following summer. The day before it reopened, the public were allowed to walk through and many thousands did.

Now join me back at that canal lock – the nearby hamlet is called Warland – and walk along to the next lock *(3 minutes).*

This is called Summit (officially Longlees lock no.36) and is the highest point of this canal as it crosses the hills between Manchester and Sowerby Bridge, near Halifax. It takes *20 minutes* to the next lock (West Summit no.37) and there is

the visitor centre mentioned in the walking route (about one and half miles from Littleborough). You can park, admire the scenery and meet the walkers. There is a loo for the disabled in the visitor centre. From this car park you can travel round most of the lake by wheelchair; there is also a special car park only for the disabled right beside the lake (on the main road).

You could drive on another *3 miles* to Milnrow where a pub called the Tim Bobbin commemorates a famous historical character, self-styled Duke of Milnrow, who wrote and illustrated lively satirical accounts of life in these parts in the eighteenth century. Many of his pictures hang on the walls of the pub together with some of his poems. There is also a pub in London named after him, although he never went near the place.

Links between routes 4 and 5

By public transport: train or bus from Littleborough to Hebden Bridge.

By car: follow the A58 up to the White House (3 miles), then turn left (B6138) to Cragg Vale and Mytholmroyd where you turn left along the A646 to Hebden Bridge (7 miles).

To walk: you follow the Rochdale canal from Littleborough to Hebden Bridge; one of these days you will be able to go by boat, but it will take longer than walking with all the locks to go through.

Booklets

To get the flavour of the area you should read:

Looking back at Littleborough by George Kelsall and Keith Parry (published by G. Kelsall, the Bookshop, Littleborough, 1981).

Tim Bobbin Lives! by Jean and Peter Bond (published by P.J. Books (Milnrow) Ltd 1986).

Survivor! The Summit Tunnel by Keith Parry (published by Keith Parry, Littleborough).

The Weighver's Seaport, The Story of Hollingworth Lake by A.W. Colligan (published by G. Kelsall, The Bookshop, Littleborough).

The Littleborough Historical Society has also published a series of booklets on history trails in the area.

Route 5

Hebden Bridge: the Calder Valley and the weavers' village

The maps for this route are Ordnance Survey Outdoor Leisure Series, South Pennines (1:25,000) and the 1:50,000 series nos. 103 and 104. The grid reference for Hebden Bridge Information Centre, in the middle of the town, is 992 271 and its phone no. is 0422 843831.

Hebden Bridge offers all the sports and hobbies of the previous routes with tennis, football, cricket, bowls, rock-climbing, archery, fishing and knur and spell. Mouse-fancying is a local speciality as is cart-driving. Do find out when the cart-driving is taking place, it is a colourful sight with the various shapes and sizes of carts, not to mention shapes and sizes of horses, racing over the hills. The Pennine Herb Society meets in the Hebden Bridge Information Centre, and there is a slalom course in the River Calder at nearby Sowerby Bridge.

Nearby, at Todmorden, you can book time on a large telescope built for amateur astronomers. There are numerous crafts represented in this area – potters, painters, woodworkers, silversmiths and a host of others. There is a nature reserve (a site of special scientific interest) to visit and a clog mill – both on walking route 1. Hebden Bridge also has two theatres, an arts festival from time to time and one of the few surviving cinemas in the area. There is a new marina on the partly restored canal, its white stonework and green and red painted boats make a colourful scene; it is also well guarded by a flock of white geese – make sure they do not mistake you for a vandal. Boating has restarted here, and you can take a short trip or hire a cruiser for a week. As elsewhere, the older settlements are on the hills, although there was a medieval wooden bridge in the valley. It was replaced by a stone structure we shall see later, just after the end of the middle ages. One district is called Old Town, in which is Automobilia, a vintage car museum (and restaurant, see below). Both the cars and the building, an old mill warehouse high in the hills, have been restored with the closest attention to detail. You can have a chauffeur-driven tour over the hills in a 1920s Morris, if you wish; you may even be able to hire a vintage car. In Old Town also is a pub called the Hare and Hounds where a game called billeting is played. This is similar to 'knur and spell', a traditional game in this area which is being revived.

Driving: a practice cart.

On another height is the old weavers' village of Heptonstall (see walking route 2) with a museum of local history and a creative writing centre. Nearby is a free range chicken farm.

On the hills to the west of Hebden Bridge, at the village of Colden, is a gallery of local art, at a garden centre called Land Farm. This remote spot can be visited by car or on foot. There is a remarkable collection of plants, pictures and sculptures, and concerts are held on the premises. Ask at the information centre for directions to get there and phone to make sure it's open. The directions include turn right onto a track by some garages, or words to that effect; do not go looking for petrol pumps as I did – these 'garages' are an untidy group of huts on the right hand side of the road. For hikers, Land Farm (grid reference 961 292) is only minutes from the Pennine Way, and a rather longer walk from Hardcastle Crags; it is near Sutcliffe's restaurant, see below.

Not to be missed is the Birchcliffe Centre, the headquarters of an organization called Pennine Heritage. This huge and ornate former Baptist chapel stands up on a hill to the north of the town; follow the steep, winding Birchcliffe Road that turns off the main road to Keighley near the town centre. The building is a monument to late Victorian religion as well as to late Victorian architecture. Built in the 1890s, in a town already well supplied with places of worship, it was designed on such a scale that the ground floor now contains a large suite of offices and the gallery makes a 300-seater theatre. The Sunday School building has been divided into 16 family bedrooms each with two beds, two bunks, a toilet and a shower. There are also social facilities inside the old premise, while a modern extension offers a room for meetings especially for groups studying the area. Pennine Heritage exists to restore and bring fresh life to the area; it publishes the Pennine magazine and numerous booklets on the South Pennines.

Knur and Spell.

If you want to wander further afield, there is Todmorden to the west where the county boundary once ran through the middle of the town hall. The roof of this classical style building has a frieze of stone carvings portraying the textile industry.

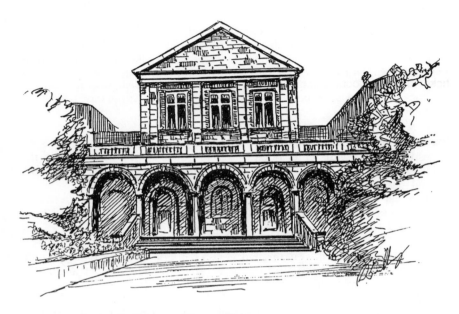

The Birchcliffe Centre: headquarters of Pennine Heritage.

Early in the last century, the member of parliament for Todmorden was Henry Fielding who introduced into the House of Commons legislation restricting the hours of work of women and children. In route 7 we shall meet Robert Collyer, one of the children who was put on the road to fame and fortune by the timely passing of an Act which not only limited his hours of work but gave him education. One of the three Fielding family houses, the Old Hall in the centre of the town, is now a restaurant, another is a boys' home and a third has been demolished to make way for a municipal swimming pool which you may like to visit.

Eight miles to the east of Hebden Bridge is Halifax, a place of weird street names like 'Top o' th' Hill' and 'Sod House Lane'. The Piece Hall ('piece' as in pieces of cloth), is the most extraordinary building between Edale and Ilkley Moor. Built as a textile market, it has stood for over 200 years upright and colourful with its 315 rooms, its columns and its arches – three stories one side and two on the other – round a huge and sloping square. The architect matched the slope, so you can walk round and find yourself on the second floor on one side and the first on the other just by keeping on the same level.

At various times of year there are bands, groups, dancers, carol singers and performers of all sorts along with a great variety of market stalls in the square of the Piece Hall. Many of the rooms are occupied by craftsmen and craftswomen; there is also a small restaurant for lunch or a snack, and along one side a museum showing the history of wool. Leading out of this is a four storey museum of the industrial history of the area with textiles, machinery, cat's eyes (which were invented in this town) and Macintosh's toffees. You enter by stamping your ticket in an old clocking-in machine and every effort is made to help you feel you are back in the industrial past, including a realistic mine with a tape describing the miner's work.

Part of the process of making cloth was to string it out over the countryside on large posts fitted with 'tenter hooks' – that is how this phrase came into the language – to hold it. The cloth was easy to steal, lying out in the fields, so a special means of execution was used for cloth thieves. No hanging, as for lesser offences like murder, the cloth stealer was guillotined. The practice ended about three hundred years ago (long before the French revolutionaries reinvented it), so you cannot see the guillotine in action. Bad luck.

If you have plenty of time and patience, you can find a replica where the old guillotine, known as the gibbet, once stood. You need to thread your way through the maze of central Halifax; it is only 10 minutes from the Piece Hall with a lot of luck; walk diagonally across the town to a road appropriately named Gibbet Street, just behind a multi-storey car park. 'You can't miss it', they'll tell you. Believe me you can; so beg, borrow or even buy a street plan from the Information Centre in the Piece Hall.

On the other side of the Piece Hall, just beyond the station is a museum of working horses which you must find irresistible. About a mile out of town, on the way to Bradford (and well served by buses, but you can walk there up a steep hill) is Shibden Hall, a fifteenth century timbered house with a great variety of carved furniture as well as a collection of carriages and some craft workshops. Another local industry is stone quarrying, the stone for London Bridge came from these parts.

How to get to Hebden Bridge

All the towns mentioned on this route are in the Metropolitan District of Calderdale. From west to east they are: Todmorden, Hebden Bridge, Mytholmroyd, Sowerby Bridge and Halifax. Calderdale boasts the largest number of inhabitants aged over 75 of any metropolitan district in the country, according to the last census. It's because they have something to live for, I understand. The district also has some of the cheapest houses, so there must be a catch somewhere. All five towns have stations on the line from Manchester to Bradford and Leeds, and trains from

Preston stop at Hebden Bridge and Halifax. There are frequent buses along the valley, and the towns are linked by the A646 road which joins the A58 just outside Halifax.

From the west the nearest motorway exit is junction 21 (as in the last route). At Littleborough turn right and follow the A58 to the top of the pass (Blackstone Edge) and beyond the White House pub, then left onto the B6138 through Cragg Vale (famous for the coin counterfeiters) to Mytholmroyd where you turn left for Hebden Bridge. From the east, turn off at exit 24 and follow the A629 (signpost Halifax) until the A6026 (to Sowerby Bridge) and the A646 to Hebden Bridge.

Accommodation, food and shopping

There are plenty of places to stay in Hebden Bridge, and opportunities for food and drink all around you. The information centre will provide a list, and I note some on the two walks. There is self-catering accommodation at Mayroyd to the east of the town.

In the village of Colden, in the hills to the west of Hebden Bridge, is the legendary Sutcliffe's. The name is that of the family that owned and ran it as a restaurant for many years. When they retired, the contents fetched £300,000 at an auction and included paintings by Rembrandt and Lely. The present proprietors have restored it to a high degree of comfort while keeping the appearance of the historic building. They welcome hikers from the Pennine Way (which passes the end of the garden) for high tea as well as gourmets to a luxury dinner. There is also bed and breakfast accommodation. Another hill overlooking Hebden Bridge, in a hamlet called Old Town, stands Automobilia – an Austrian style restaurant and vintage car museum combined. Another restaurant I recommend for a special occasion is Sacha's in nearby Todmorden. Making effective use of the interior of the historic Oddfellows Hall is this Italian style restaurant, the proprietor comes from Malta. In the centre of Hebden Bridge are numerous teashops (but if you like a smoke-free atmosphere go to the Watergate), pubs (I liked the Railway, but cannot pretend to have tried them all) a Greek restaurant serving an excellent meze and a new hotel that is on the main road, but reasonably soundproofed with double glazing; it serves a salad bar lunch.

In nearby Sowerby Bridge is the Ash Tree, a pub which also contains an Indonesian Restaurant; the cooking, the decor and the music are all genuine; you just have to find time to visit one of the limited number of Indonesian restaurants in this country.

Hebden Bridge also has a wide range of shops. You can buy your leisure clothes here – Hebden cords. You can also find a range of souvenirs at the Bridge Mill; there is an above average health food shop in Market Street, and much else.

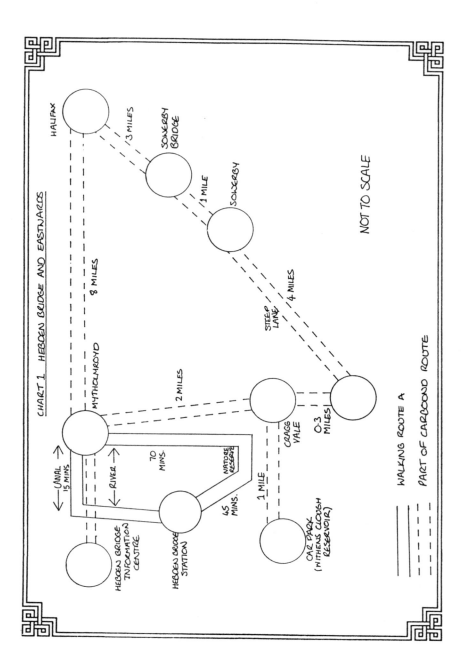

CHART 1 HEBDEN BRIDGE AND EASTWARDS

NOT TO SCALE

HALIFAX

SOWERBY BRIDGE — 3 MILES

SOWERBY — 1 MILE

STEEP LANE — 4 MILES

MYTHOLMROYD — 8 MILES

CRAGG VALE — 2 MILES

0·3 MILES

← CANAL 15 MINS →

← RIVER →

70 MINS.

NATURE RESERVE

45 MINS.

1 MILE

HEBDEN BRIDGE INFORMATION CENTRE

HEBDEN BRIDGE STATION

CAR PARK (WITHENS CLOUGH RESERVOIR)

——— WALKING ROUTE A

– – – PART OF CAR/COACH ROUTE

99

Special events

This is an area for special events with colourful ceremonies of ancient origin, sometimes revived with great attention to detail. In Hebden Bridge there is the Pace Egg play on Good Friday; in Sowerby Bridge is the Rushbearing ceremony in September (revived in 1977 after an interval of 71 years). This lasts throughout the weekend with long processions over different parts of the area on the Saturday and the Sunday.

There is much else to see and do in this enterprising little town with its ancient ceremonies and modern festivals, but let's get walking. On this route I'm suggesting two walks, both circular and providing the maximum of interest and variety. The information centre will sell you bookets with plenty of other suggestions.

Walking route A: Broad Head and Walkley's Cloggs *Remember that there is a deliberate mistake on one of these routes, see quiz at end of book.*

This route gives less than two hours' walking time but you may want to stop or divert on the way, so allow at least three. Start at Hebden Bridge station but, if you come by car don't risk the wrath of British Rail by parking there. Park in town and walk to the station – a few minutes east of the town, along the main road to Halifax and on the right. It once won a prize for the best restored station. If you wonder how, take another look at the chunky stone and the canopy supported by columns sometimes decorated with flowers.

Springing to action, after contemplating the decaying flower baskets, you walk down a slope beyond the station, turn sharp right and under the railway. On the other side take the centre of three tracks *(2 minutes)* – the one ahead that goes upwards. In another *10 minutes* the path turns right past some restored cottages named Wood Top (if you can see poles carrying cables with street lamps attached, you're all right). Immediately fork left, passing some old houses called Shroggs, then down hill (for a change – *4 minutes*). *2 minutes* later (after passing round restored a farmhouse on the left) find a stile on the right immediately before a bridge that crosses a little stream. Follow the track more or less straight up the hillside, deviating slightly to the right for a fence round a young copse, but not turning off. This is muddy and steep, and brings you up to a small pylon beside a stream that may be dry *(10 minutes)*. *2 minutes* later, the path joins a track, there are some cottages on the right. Then sharp left. After another *2 minutes* go through a gate, cross a shallow ford and pass a farm on the right. Keep parallel with electric pylons on the left. The path goes through a space in the wall and then keeps parallel to the wall until you reach a little gate where you turn right and keep along a double walled track. Continue on this course until the wall on the right finishes *(10 minutes)*.

A prize-winning station.

Stop and look round. You have only been walking for three quarters of an hour, but you have already passed through a great variety, from the woods at the bottom, with several aged oak trees, to the varied shrubs and trees as you scrambled up the grass bank to the open moorland which lies ahead. You can see across Calderdale to the wooded valleys to the north that will be explored on the next walk; to the right are places with names like Mytholmroyd ('My', as in 'My', don't say 'Mi') and Luddendenfoot.

At the end of one wall, turn half left and take a path which follows the base stones of another, broken, wall. The head of the valley is in front of you – do *not* turn right or left – and eventually (in *12 minutes)* find a steep path down to the left beside a post that stands just beyond a dilapilated wall. This post used to have a notice on it telling you that this is a nature reserve. If it has not been replaced at least look for the post – make sure you follow the correct path down.

101

I am now going to take you through a nature reserve and in a circle back to Hebden Bridge. But you have a choice here. You can stay on the path you are on and walk over to the next valley southwards, a very thickly wooded valley called Cragg Vale. With such an expressive name, there must be a story – and indeed there is. A little over 200 years ago Cragg Vale was the haunt of a group of coin counterfeiters. For their raw material, they ground the edges of gold coins which they then put back into circulation – milled edges were introduced to make this more difficult. With the grindings they made 3,500 Real Portuguese coins which were easy to sell to traders locally and in London. Survey the valley and picture all the activity needed for this very private enterprise, not to mention the channels of communication needed to move the coins to and from the City of London.

There is a sequel. Officialdom eventually caught up with them, naturally, and many were hanged – some for coining, others for murdering a customs officer who was tracking them. You will be able to stand on the grave of the leader at Heptonstall on the next walk.

If you do make this deviation, you can have a drink at the Hinchliffe Arms and look at some of the coiners' tackle and the coins they made (you may be able to see some more on the next walk). You can also see Bell House, home of David Hartley, the leader of the gang. It overlooks the nature reserve and is marked on the map. If you decide not to go round by Cragg Vale, go through the nature reserve owned by the Yorkshire Naturalists Trust, (phone: 0904 59570; I'm sure they will be glad of your support). It is a public footpath, but do keep quiet and do not touch the plants. You are now back in woodland, and among ancient oaks again.

The path goes steeply down and winds through the woods for *10 minutes*. Leave this path when you see a wooden stairway on the right which leads to a stone path and then to a farm track which brings you to the end of the nature reserve *(5 minutes)*.

Cross the tracks here and follow the one that leads down the valley, turning sharp left onto another farm track in *5 minutes*. In another *10 minutes* turn right and past some houses. Do not take the path which descends quickly to the valley. *5 minutes* later the track seems to be expiring in someone's yard, but you will find a small gate on your right. Pass through this and follow the footpath over a stile and onto a partly overgrown stone track *(2 minutes)*.

Stop a minute and look round. On your right across the valley are some grim looking huts for chickens; below you is the industrial town of Mytholmroyd (once the scene of a long sit-in, when a factory making blankets was taken over and production moved out of the country). Unless fashions have changed, you will notice a taste for light blue on the houses below you, tin town the district is called. Press on, it's all downhill now.

Over another stile, through a wall and steep down through an avenue of trees to a road in the suburbs of the town. *(10 minutes).* Turn right and immediately left and you will soon be faced with a street sign that says Nest Estate East where you cross the railway by a footbridge, at a T junction and turn left *(5 minutes).* After another *3 minutes,* just before Linden Rd, turn right down some steps and cross a river by an old stone bridge which brings you to the main road. At this point you are at a bus stop with frequent services to Hebden Bridge if you have walked enough; but don't give up easily, you only have a short distance and on the flat.

Across the road is a group of well-restored cottages called The Square. You pass these cottages and cross (on their right as you face them) a small field with newly planted trees and on to the canal towpath at a lock called Broadbottom Lock no. 7. After *5 minutes* the towpath comes near to the road where a Clog Mill stands on the other side.

Do spare a few minutes to visit the last working clog mill in the country. Since it is up for sale as this book goes to press, there may be changes by the time you read this. At present you can see all the processes in the commercial manufacture of clogs, although you have to get used to watching the workmen through glass barriers. No doubt these have been put up for safety reasons and at least you are able to wander around freely without a guide, so don't grumble. Go upstairs for refreshments (even if the description 'licensed restaurant' does not live up to the hopes it raises). You can also buy some colourful, decorated clogs, ideal for dancing or growing crocuses in.

After leaving the Clog Mill, rejoin the towpath and *8 minutes* later find yourself back at the station.

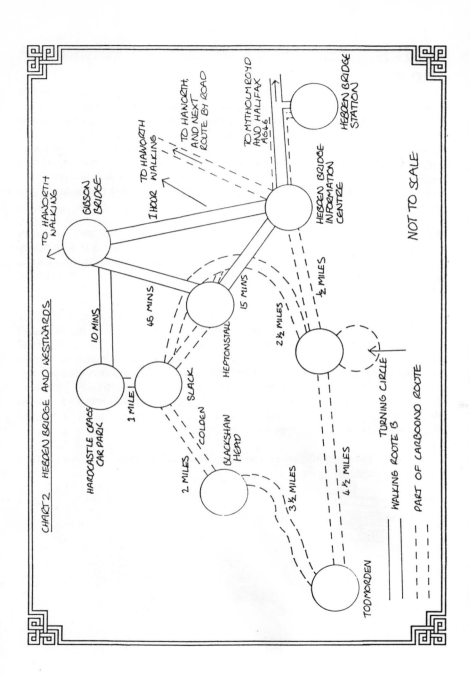

CHART 2 HEBDEN BRIDGE AND WESTWARDS

NOT TO SCALE

GIBSON BRIDGE

TO HAWORTH WALKING

1 HOUR

TO HAWORTH WALKING

TO HAWORTH AND NEXT ROUTE BY ROAD

TO MYTHOLMROYD AND HALIFAX A646

HEBDEN BRIDGE STATION

HEBDEN BRIDGE INFORMATION CENTRE

10 MINS

45 MINS

15 MINS

HEPTONSTALL

2½ MILES

½ MILES

HARDCASTLE CRAGS CAR PARK

1 MILE

SLACK

COLDEN

2 MILES

BLACKSHAW HEAD

3½ MILES

4½ MILES

TURNING CIRCLE

WALKING ROUTE B

PART OF CARBOUND ROUTE

TODMORDEN

104

Walking route B: Hardcastle Craggs and the weavers' village

Walk A took us south and east, walk B (also circular) will take us north and west. The walking time is just over *two hours,* but allow four as there is much to see.

Start from the station again and walk along the main road. You pass a suburb called Machpelah, with an old furniture factory now used by a software company. Facing you at the traffic lights is the information centre, providing not only a mine of informatic ı, but also regular exhibitions which are worth a visit in their own right. Sometimes you can tour the area in your imagination by walking round a series of pictures which sum up the spirit and inspiration of these hills. The road that goes north from the lights is called Bridge Gate and a few yards along on the left is a car park; if you are coming by car, it will be full but there are plenty of others and they are well signposted. Just past the car park is an old packhorse bridge.

A pack horse bridge.

Have a look at this bridge which represents design and craftsmanship from nearly 500 years ago; it replaced a medieval timber structure. Carry on to the next bridge *(10 minutes* walking time from the station), note the Bridge Mill (now shops and a restaurant) on your right and cross the bridge (St. George's Street) of nineteenth century iron work. Turn right into Valley Road and follow until you cross another bridge in Victoria Road *(5 minutes)*. Here you can see Nutclough Mill on your right. This large mill was a pioneer of cooperative production. Pennine Heritage saved it from destruction and have restored it; there are workshops and a visitor centre is planned. The whole provides a powerful spectacle from where you should now be standing.

Continue as Victoria Road swings left with a children's playground on the left. Pass the site of a demolished mill on your right. At the end of this you turn right before a restored factory and immediately left, crossing the river (Hebden Water) yet again, this time on another packhorse bridge *(5 minutes)*. Note the design of this bridge, a work of art in itself. Turn right, through a gap in the wall, and follow the path across a meadow and beside the river. You can fish here, with a permit from the information centre; you can also see a grey wagtail, a small yellow-looking bird which darts from rock to rock.

The path goes by a cricket ground, some allotments and a bowling green. Leaving a footbridge on your right, go round to the back of the clubhouse and on to a track *(5 minutes)*. When the main track forks right, fork left and walk up a hill which brings you (in another *5 minutes)* to a free-range chicken farm. This is very free-range, you see the chickens all over the path and in the forest. Try a conversation with them, they respond well. When I asked why they were not caught by the foxes, I was told that they return to their sheds at night. The same, it seems, is also true of the rabbits that are bred here. Occasionally in the summer the proprietor takes parties round the farm and the packing station, so ring up if you have an interested group.

At the far end of the farm you come, in *3 minutes,* to some well-restored buildings where you turn sharp back to the left and then right up some stone steps. At the top you turn right *(2 minutes)*. In another *3 minutes,* cross the Calderdale Way and follow a path through the woods. You can see a river and a dam far below on your right. *15 minutes* later the path winds up hill between some hostel buildings and up some concrete steps after which you turn right.

The path now descends steeply to the river *(3 minutes)*, which you cross on stepping stones – to be avoided when they are covered in ice. On the far side is a National Trust sign which reads 'Hardcastle Crags.' The path follows up the valley and brings you, in *12 minutes,* to Gibson Bridge where there is an old mill and a toll house. You can stop here and look round after walking for an hour.

Mr.Gibson, the millowner, was a benefactor to Heptonstall Church – 'paid 'em out of the sweated labour of children,' one of the locals told me.

From here there are four choices.

- You can follow me back to Hebden Bridge by a different route through the weavers' village of Heptonstall.

- You can walk up to the Hardcastle Crags car park and join the carbound party (you start on the same path).

- You can walk further up the valley (turn right across bridge) and then come back to join the route.

- You can turn round and follow a well-marked track straight back to Hebden Bridge.

The route crosses Gibson Bridge and turns left on the far side of the river to a track that climbs under the trees for *8 minutes* until it reaches a bend which doubles back to the right with a low wall on the left. Keep on this right hand track if you want to go up to the car park (*10 minutes* away).

The route turns left at this bend onto a narrow path through woods and up to some stone steps near a fence (*12 minutes*). Keep alongside the fence and pass through a gap in a wall (*3 minutes*) and another gap (*2 minutes*). Then left and immediately right, admiring the rock formation and taking care of a precipice on the left. In *5 minutes* you reach a small gate; do not go through, but turn left and along a fence. Here there is a view of the river, way below at the bottom of the gorge, and of some more rock formations. In *5 minutes*, cross a wall by some steps, and follow beside the fence which is now on the left.

The field you are crossing was covered in huts 80 years ago when it was called Dawson City and a small army of navvies lived in crowded and spartan conditions while building reservoirs in the hills nearby. A railway took them and their materials to work, crossing much higher up the valley on a trestle bridge. The remains of the supports for the bridge can still be seen.

On your left across the valley is Shackleton Hill: the name had links with the family of Shackleton the explorer. Due north from where you stand is another deep wooded valley with waterfalls. Its name, Crimsworth Dean, raises high hopes which are completely fulfilled; the shortest way to walk to Haworth (the next route) is up that valley. To the north west of Crimsworth Dean, the Moors are owned by Lord Saville and reserved for shooting parties. This is a piece of forbidden Britain. On a hill to the north west stands a war memorial.

On the skyline to the east is Mount Skip; you can make out the buildings of a mink farm there.

Cross a road and follow a path across some meadows; then follow along a walled path, arriving in *10 minutes* in the middle of the village of Heptonstall.

Heptonstall: the weavers' village.

This is an old weavers' village which was at one time nearly deserted. It is now reinhabited but has remained much as it was, a chance to see a village locked into history. Wander round but respect the privacy of the inhabitants.

A celebrated building is the Cloth Hall. Built over 400 years ago, at the end of the reign of King Henry VIII, it claims to be the oldest market for woollen pieces in Yorkshire. It is now a private house.

You enter from a side street and cross into the Weavers' Square, surrounded by houses once occupied by weaving families. In front of you are two churches, one in ruins. The ruined church goes back over 700 years, but most of the remains are not that old. It was damaged in a storm in 1847 and a new one was built nearby. In the old churchyard, near the entrance to the ruins, is the grave of David Hartley who was executed in 1770 for coin counterfeiting. Some of the equipment used for the counterfeiting is in the Museum in the Old Grammar School just outside the churchyard; some, we have already said, is in the Hinchliffe Arms at Cragg Vale.

Have a look at the rest of the museum and then wander out to view the newer church. There are concerts here on some weekends. In the new cemetery on the other side of the church is the grave of the poetess Sylvia Plath, wife of Ted Hughes, now poet laureate, who was born in the Calder Valley and lived nearby. On the grave is one simple line from Sylvia Plath's poetry: 'even amidst fierce flame the golden lotus can be planted.' She died at the age of 31.

The house where she and Ted Hughes lived is only ten minutes walk away and is now a creative writing centre. You go there by walking back to the Piece Hall, and turning left along the road through the village. You will find the Lumb Bank sign ('Arvon Foundation') on your left, the house stands at the bottom of a steep track. If you have hopes of writing fiction or poetry, do apply for a place on a five day course here. You will be helped to develop your skills by experienced writers.

Lumb Bank: creative writing centre

Across the road from the Cloth Hall is the Cross Inn which serves Timothy Taylor's beers, a local (Keighley) brew and one of the tastiest in the country. You can also get lunch here.

An old inhabitant I met told me of his forefathers who wove cloth in this area. He talked about the 'offcumdens', the foreigners from countries like Manchester and Leeds, who had come to live in these parts. (The local paper calls them 'offcomers'). Apparently these outsiders have pushed up house prices, but if you live almost anywhere else in the country, you will think they have not pushed very hard. Their more serious offence is to try to have a say in local affairs which, my friend assured me, should be left to those born here. He spoke fiercely, too, of the greed of the mill-owners and the invasion of the dam-building navvies, long since disappeared.

Not far away, at the other end of a car park whose narrow entrance is a few yards downhill from the Cross Inn, is an octagonal methodist chapel. This is one of the few places of worship built by the methodists during John Wesley's lifetime and has been in continuous use since. He usually preached in Anglican churches or in the open air, but he may well have preached here. It is also said that he stipulated the octagonal design.

To continue the walk back to Hebden Bridge – you can go by bus if you wish, but it's all downhill now – find your way back to the museum, and go down the steps on the far side, turning left and along a street called West Laithe. At the end, turn left *(2 minutes)* and then right by a row of garages. Keep along the track, it passes between two walls and note the monument which stands on the highest point across the valley.

Stoodley Pike is a landmark for miles around, and for walkers on the Pennine Way. It has had a chequered career. The site is over 1300 feet above sea level and has probably been a centre of activity through the ages. The present monument goes back to 1814, when it was decided to put up a memorial to peace after the defeat of Napoleon. Building stopped abruptly when war broke out again, but was continued after the Battle of Waterloo. Some years later the Pike was struck by lightning and in 1854 it finally collapsed just before the start of another War (the Crimean). Two years' after that it was rebuilt in memory of yet another peace. It failed to fall down again during the conflicts of the twentieth century. Strange.

Back to earth and steep down for *2 minutes* to Hell Hole Rocks, designed for climbers; follow the path round them and down into the valley. Before you go too far, look down and see how a road, a railway, a canal and a river jostle one another in the narrow space below. This is typical of the Pennines where four methods of transport followed the rivers and all are cramped for space. Even the roads are comparatively modern; the ancient roads followed the hill tops. If you travel on the railway, it seems as if you are on the underground there are so many tunnels.

Stoodley Pike.

In *15 minutes* you join a road, turn right. Note the top to bottom houses, a feature of these parts. The houses across the road you are now walking down were not built as four storied, but as two rows of two storied. The top houses have front doors opening on to the street you are on, and the bottom houses have front doors opening on to a street below and on the other side. In this way, they used the natural contours of the land and packed as many people into the narrow valley as possible. Most of the flat space in the bottom was taken by factories after the river, the road, the canal and the railway had had their pick.

After passing the houses, and *2 minutes* after joining the road, turn left through a gap in the wall and down a series of steps. *4 minutes* later go under a bridge which joins two parts of a mill and turn left along the main road. This brings you back to the centre of Hebden Bridge in *5 minutes* and the station in another *5*.

The carbound route

You cannot follow the walkers all the way but there is much for you in this area and I am taking you a longer route than usual. Leave the car park you found in the town and head west across the traffic lights by the Information Centre and across the next lights. Almost immediately, and after a garage, you come to a 'turning circle' – a feature of these parts to prevent traffic jams caused by sharp right turns *(half mile)*. You go round this circle and back the way you came to the lights where you fork left (signpost Heptonstall). There is a car park on the edge of the village which is near the end of the walkers' second route.

Note: traffic is prohibited in Heptonstall except for access. So only go to the car park if you intend to visit the village. Otherwise drive round and rejoin the road on the other side at the village of Slack.

Whether you go to Heptonstall or not, drive through Slack and fork right at the end of the village *(2.5 miles* from turning circle). In *1 mile,* the Hardcastle Crags car park (National Trust) is on your right. Here is a chance to admire the view and perhaps meet the walkers.

On leaving the car park go back to the fork in Slack *(1 mile)* and turn sharp right. The next village is Colden (the site of a restaurant and art gallery already mentioned) and on to Blackshaw Head *(2 miles)* where you turn left – not the first sharp left turn, but the next. The turning is not signposted but is just beyond the Shoulder of Mutton Inn; follow the road, keeping left twice as it winds its way steeply down to Todmorden *(3.5 miles).* After looking round another historic Pennine place, drive back to Hebden Bridge *(4.5 miles)* along the main road and through the town. On the other side is the Clog Mill (walking route one), after which you come to Mytholmroyd. Keep straight on, bypass Sowerby Bridge and enter Halifax *(8 miles).* There is a large car park on the far side of the town by the station.

On the return journey follow the signposts into Sowerby Bridge *(3 miles)* and through the town following the A58 towards Ripponden. The Rochdale canal joins the Calder and Hebble navigation at Sowerby Bridge, and there are wharfs full of colourful longboats here; the towpath is being restored to a standard that can take wheelchairs.

After crossing over the canal and river and under the railway (in that order) you take the first right (signpost Sowerby) which brings you up to the old village of Sowerby *(1 mile)* – an example of an old settlement on the hills, with a town that grew up in the industrial revolution (Sowerby Bridge) in the valley. Have a look at the church, and then keep right (signpost Steep Lane). On reaching Steep Lane, keep left and follow the road across the hills – straight ahead at the next crossroads and keeping left later – until it eventually joins the road from Littleborough to Mytholmroyd in the beginning of the valley that leads to Cragg Vale *(4 miles)*. Turn sharp right at this point and very sharp left in a little over a *mile* when you come down into the valley. This turn is hard to find, so watch out; you can see the turrets on top of the church tower sticking through the trees on your left, you then see a road sign indicating that the road is swinging to the right. Here you take this sharp left turn into a narrow road, pass Cragg Vale church, the Hinchliffe Arms and the entrance to Cragg Hall where once lived the local millowner, Mr. Hinchliffe Hinchliffe (yes, that really was his name, his tomb is in the churchyard). Follow up the valley to a car park on the edge of the moors near a large reservoir called Withens Clough. In this car park, you stand between the thick forests of the valley and the tough grasses of the moors. 'You could not have designed a valley better,' I was told in the Hinchliffe Arms. The valley is also a fine example of nature overcoming the works of man. A solitary, high and unusually thin chimney is all that remains of a once thriving industry now buried in shrubland and forest. Of all the shops in the village, only the post office remains and there are rumours that that may close. An hourly minibus links the village with Mytholmroyd and Hebden Bridge.

In the Hinchliffe Arms is a collection of coining equipment and examples of genuine coins beside the forgeries – demonstrating vividly the craftsmanship of the counterfeiters. There is also a copy of a notice about the counterfeiters giving their descriptions – 'thinnish visaged and of a fair complexion . . . indifferently dressed.' What a photofit.

From the reservoir back to the main road is *1 mile*, down into Mytholmroyd another *2*, and from there, after turning left, another *mile* to Hebden Bridge.

Link to next route

Haworth (route 6) is between 8 and 9 miles away.

By bus: service 500 from Hebden Bridge.

By car: drive along the A6033 northwards out of Hebden Bridge (signpost Keighley), turn left at Oxenhope (signpost Haworth) where you pass the terminus of the Keighley and Worth Valley Railway (seven miles). In half a mile, turn right at T junction. There is a car park this side of the old town of Haworth and another at the end of the bypass. The latter is 8.7 miles from Hebden Bridge.

To walk. There are two routes. A long hilly walk takes you along the path followed by route A to Gibson's Bridge and then straight on up the valley (either side) to the Pennine Way at the head. Follow this by the two reservoirs (Lower and Upper Walshaw), turning off at Top Withins along the well defined path to

Haworth. The other route is shorter and much less strenuous. Start on route A, but turn right up Crimsworth Dene (National Trust) and then follow Haworth old road past the Lee Shaw reservoir and into Haworth by a road from the reservoir (I have taken a bicycle by that route, but it is not possible to ride all the way).

Booklets

Dozens of fascinating booklets have been produced on this area – just wander round the Birchcliffe Centre or the information centre. I have chosen for you four very different ones which I found most interesting.

Setting the Scene by David Fletcher, published by Pennine Heritage.

Coiners' Chronicle by Bruce Holdsworth, published by Peacock Books, Mytholmroyd.

Heptonstall Trail, published by Calder Civic Trust.

The Calderdale Way, published by the Calderdale Way Association, 56 pages packed with an exceptional variety of detail.

Route 6:

The Land of the Brontës

Haworth, the home of the Brontës, is the best known and most touristic place in this book. If you are allergic to mass rallies, keep away at weekends, especially in the summer; even in winter, the place can be crowded.

The map for this route is the 1:25,000 South Pennines, Ordnance Survey Outdoor Leisure Series, as for Hebden Bridge. The grid reference for Haworth Church is 030372. There is a tourist information centre in the old town, phone 0535 42329, and a visitor centre at Wycoller.

Haworth is built on two levels, like Hebden Bridge and Sowerby Bridge and many other towns in this area. The old town up on the hill, and the newer town in the valley. You will want to spend most of your time on the hills, but you must visit the Keighley and Worth Valley Railway; one of the most enterprising of the private railways, it includes a museum, a large stock of locomotives, some prize-winning stations, locations for films, and initiatives like Pullmans with gourmet meals and Santa specials at Christmas time. You can also join the society.

Haworth does not boast any festivals. It hardly needs to; life is one long festival and you can see morris dancing and other street displays at various times of year. Oxenhope has a straw race at the beginning of July.

Apart from the railway which came late in the railway era, the first ten reasons for visiting Haworth can be given by repeating the word Brontë ten times. You can find books, leaflets and pictures by the score in the Information Centre, the bookshops and the Brontë museum that tell the story of the family, but let me just remind you.

The father and mother of the Brontës were both offcomers in this area. Mr. Brontë was the son of an Irish peasant named Brunty; he changed his surname while a student at Cambridge as a result of his admiration for Lord Nelson, who was Duke of Brontë. That's where the name comes from. Mrs. Brontë came from Cornwall.

They moved to the parsonage at Haworth in 1820 with five daughters and a son. The old man survived to run the church for 41 years, but his wife died a year after they arrived and within 25 years all six children were dead. The two oldest girls died at 10 and 11. The dreadful school to which they went is described in Jane Eyre along with the death of one of them. The brother (named Branwell, after his mother's maiden name) was a drug addict, you could buy opium in the local chemist's shop in those days; he died in his thirties. Branwell was a popular young man and a regular at the Black Bull where he entertained the visitors.

The Keighley and Worth Valley Railway.

The other three children all became famous novelists and all died young. Emily wrote Wuthering Heights and lived 30 years, Anne wrote Agnes Grey and The Tenant of Wildfell Hall and lived to be 29 and Charlotte, who wrote Jane Eyre and Shirley, died at the age of 39.

But there is more than this mixture of tragedy and outspoken, pioneer feminist novels to their story. There is a struggle for careers for women, there is romance (Charlotte had an affair with a married employer and Branwell had a string of affairs) and much else besides Charlotte's marriage to a curate apparently *because* he was scorned by her father.

Haworth: Main Street and the Black Bull.

The Brontë Museum is in the old parsonage where the family lived. You can tour the rooms they occupied, but you can also see samples of their work – drawings and paintings as well as writings. The Museum also houses the headquarters of the Brontë Society together with a collection of manuscripts and secondary material about the family. The collection has been put together over the last hundred years and is consulted by a wide variety of people from scholars with international reputations to casual tourists. In the museum bookshop all the writings of the sisters are on sale, including their poems and childhood writings.

The reputation of the Brontës makes Haworth interesting to visitors from almost anywhere in the world. The museum is visited by nearly a quarter of a million people a year. There were 213,000 in 1985, almost exactly five times the number who came here in 1960, but by no means a record for recent years. The visitor's book in 1986 contained the names of visitors from six countries (Belgium, Canada, France, Germany, Ireland and the United States) in just two days in *late October*. The museum should receive an export award. Incidentally if that number of people visited the museum, how many do you suppose visited Haworth? I guess it must be nearly a million; I cannot believe that more than one in four actually go inside the museum.

As I write, efforts are being made to restore the inside of the house to a condition as similar as possible to that which the Brontës knew; without the diseases they suffered from, I presume. Fortunately Branwell painted himself in bed, so it is possible to reconstruct his bedroom. Similarly the wallpaper is being replaced by designs the family chose and the kitchen organized as they had it.

Many of Branwell's pictures hang in the museum, a particularly effective one is of a Mr. James Fletcher of Skipton. The most famous of the pictures is the one in which he painted himself with his three sisters and then painted himself out leaving a curious gap; this is in the National Portrait Gallery. There are also some pictures by Charlotte. Another famous novelist (Mrs. Gaskell) wrote Charlotte's life story.

The town survives as it was, with the old buildings and the cobbled street. The church was mostly rebuilt by old Brontë's successor, and contains the Brontë graves, including that of the relation (Aunt Branwell) who brought them up.

The town is a tourist centre with the Brontë legend on every side. There is also a museum of childhood where you can gaze at dolls or play trains.

How to get to Haworth

By train: come via Leeds. There are trains to Keighley, a station on the line to Skipton from Leeds and Bradford. From the north or north west you can also come via Skipton. There are buses from Halifax, Skipton and Hebden Bridge.

By car: from the south follow the route to Hebden Bridge (less than 9 miles away, see route 5) and follow the A6033 (signpost to Keighley) until Oxenhope where Haworth is signposted to the left. You cannot take your car into the old town, but there are large car parks each side of it.

Accommodation, food and shopping

The countryside around Haworth is full of bed and breakfast accommodation, and there are hotels in the town and not far away. The information centre has a list which can be read in one of the windows when the centre is closed. Look for Keighley if searching the yellow pages.

The Old Hall serves good food and drink (both in the restaurant and the bar). It also has bed and breakfast accommodation. Parts of the present house are very old; it once had tunnels for escape in times of religious persecution. In front of it was the village green where a ducking stool was provided to punish naggers – a useful facility, you might think, but brutal too. You could die of the ducking.

Haworth: The Old Hall.

There are plenty of cafes in Main Street (that is its name) and pubs including the Black Bull which serves meals, including teas, and is the place for the family at almost any time. The King's Arms also has good food and a warm welcome. At the top of the old village is the Weavers, one of the outstanding restaurants in the area. You need to book.

There are numerous souvenir shops in the town; some sell relics of the textile industry which you may prefer to anaemic pictures of the Brontës (their monuments are their books not their faces). There are also millshops (converted mills) in and around the town which sell everything for the home from furniture to towels. The Information Centre has a list of them and can tell you where to find them. Local craftspeople, and some not so local, sell hand-made textiles as well as pottery, carvings and pictures. The shops in Haworth are mixed, a homely lot; fascinating relics of the textile industry jostle with a lot of junk for the attention of the tourists. Above all it is a place for the hand-made, from pullovers to chocolates there are local products (some made in Keighley or Ilkley) as well as the arts and crafts. At the top of Main Street is an artists' field study centre which offers accommodation.

I am suggesting one long walk this time, starting past the church and the parsonage where the Brontës lived and died.

The Walking route: Haworth to Wycoller

Remember there is an intentional mistake, see the quiz at the end of the book.

This is a long walk across the hills. You can turn back at several points; if you make it to the other end, you can get a bus back.

Start from Haworth station, if you come by train (Keighley and Worth Valley Railway, only available during the summer and some weekends during the winter) or bus (regular service from Keighley), and cross the railway by the footbridge; walk straight up to the higher part of the town crossing the bypass and swinging right on the way. Find the church on your left (15 minutes). If you come by car, follow the road up into one of the car parks beside the old town. Do find a car park. Many people park in the street – a mean gesture to save a very small contribution to the local well-being. The carbound route starts from the car park at the end of the bypass, near the top of the town and across the road from the police station.

Inside the church, the grave of the Brontë family (all except Anne who is buried in Scarborough) is at the east end on the right. You will easily find the details. Coming out of the church, turn westwards, that is left at the north west entrance, the far corner from the Brontë memorial. You are in a narrow street and soon pass the Sunday School building, where Charlotte Brontë taught, on your right and the parsonage on your left. This is where the famous family lived and is now a museum maintained by the Brontë society. It is certainly not to be missed, but you have a long way to go today, so why not stay overnight and visit the museum tomorrow? It will take you at least two hours to go round and you will probably want to pay a subscription to the Brontë Society before you have finished; the oldest literary society in Britain, it will be celebrating its centenary in the 1990s.

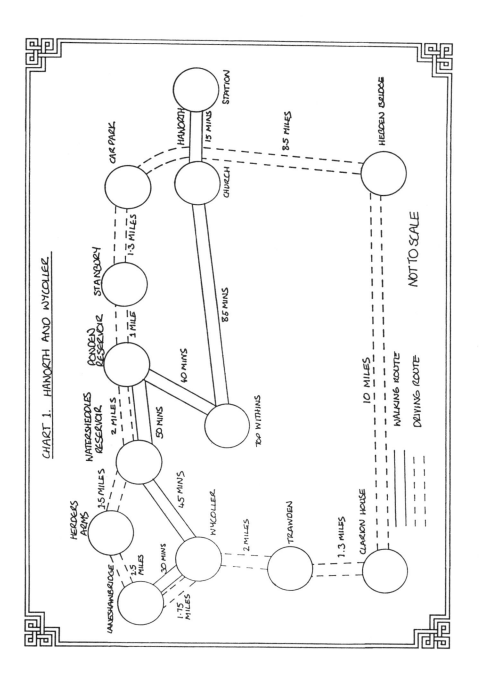

CHART 1. HAWORTH AND WYCOLLER

STATION
HAWORTH
15 MINS
CAR PARK
CHURCH
8.5 MILES
HEBDEN BRIDGE
1.3 MILES
STANBURY
1 MILE
PONDEN RESERVOIR
40 MINS
8.5 MINS
TOP WITHINS
WATERSHEDDLES RESERVOIR
2 MILES
50 MINS
HERDERS ARMS
1.5 MILES
45 MINS
WYCOLLER
2.5 MILES
10 MINS
2 MILES
TRAWDEN
1.3 MILES
CLARION HOUSE
10 MILES
WALKING ROUTE
DRIVING ROUTE
LANESHAWBRIDGE
1.75 MILES
NOT TO SCALE

121

The home of the Brontës.

Leave the vicarage on your left and follow along a lane and across a field to a gap in a wall where you join a road. Keep on the left hand side, fork left (Cemetery Road), cross the road and up a footpath on the right hand side *(7 minutes* from church). This runs beside the road and up to a layby, just before the cemetery entrance on the left, after which walk along the road *(3 minutes)*. *10 minutes* later, cross another road (Oxenhope to Stanbury) and onto a track, soon passing through a gate.

On the right you look down at the Lower Laithe reservoir; in front are the hills that form the Pennine skyline. There is heather all around; the little yellow flowers are oddly called black medick, there are also some bird's foot trefoil (of the pea family, my flower book tells me) and tormentil which are yellow too.

Follow this path to Brontë Bridge *(20 minutes)*. You can bring a pushchair this far, although there are some steps towards the end. The rocks are good for

through a gap in the wall, over a wooden bridge and stop. You are crossing the River Worth, and surely need a rest in this magic place.

When refreshed, follow the path over a stile and up the valley, crossing another 3 stiles and following the stream up to a stone marking a boundary in *(10 minutes)*. You are now standing on the frontier between Yorkshire and Lancashire (and between the City of Bradford and the Borough of Pendle). A notice tells you that this place is unique, surprising and secluded (it would, wouldn't it?).

Put your passport away and cross yet another stile; I did tell you to leave your dog and your pushchair behind, you will rupture yourself lifting them over all these stiles. Follow the path up to the Watersheddles Reservoir. Walk between the reservoir and the road. At the end of the reservoir, cross a wooden bridge and another stile and turn left (*10 minutes*). There is a car park nearby if you have some friends to meet; there are no buses on this road.

It is now three hours walking time from Haworth, but you will have taken longer and time will be getting on; take heart it's mostly downhill to Wycoller.

Cross another wooden bridge and follow a fence on your left for *5 minutes* and cross a stile. Right and left, and follow the path as it meanders over the moor and down to another wooden bridge. Then straight up and turn left along a farm track *(8 minutes)*. Continue along this track as it winds downhill and then up again. Right at the top of the hill *(10 minutes* – footpath sign to Wycoller), then downhill towards the valley. Way up on your right you can see the road and an old pub, the Crofters – worth a visit sometime, good food. A bird you may see here is the Wheatear. This lean, elegantly shaped bird, with grey back, black wings, pale breast and a white rump which is obvious when it flies, sits on the fence, often letting you come close to admire him (or perhaps it's a her).

After passing through a gate, with a stream on the right and a farm on the left *(8 minutes),* continue following the farm track down the valley, crossing the stream three times, and keeping right just before the third crossing (another *8 minutes),* when the left hand path goes to Trawden – worth visiting, but on another day. There is a lot of red campion decorating the edges of the stream in late summer. The stream is Smithy Clough which leads into Wycoller Beck just before you reach the Clam Bridge *(3 minutes).*

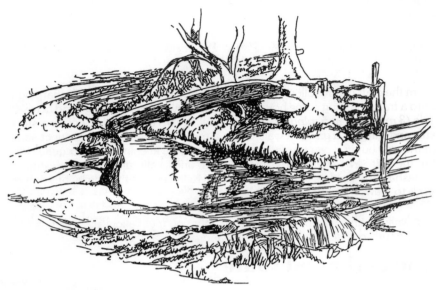

Clam Bridge, Wycoller.

Stop and have a good look at one of the oldest forms of bridge building known to man and imagine our ancestors laboriously manoeuvering this huge stone into position. Opinions differ, but I guess it has been here for more than three thousand years. Note the narrow part on the far side of the stream which give the bridge its distinctive shape and its name.

Another *3 minutes* will bring you to the hamlet of Wycoller where you will find two more old bridges and a ford. Evidently this once stood on a main highway, now lost. Arrows from long before Christ have been found here.

A few years ago Wycoller – once a handloom weavers' village – was uninhabited; now the cottages are reoccupied but the Hall remains in ruins, a relic of a mansion (said to be the Ferndean Manor of Jane Eyre). The seventeenth century barn has an exhibition of the history of the area, and a warden who can tell you the local history.

Further on one of the old buildings is a craft centre and a cafe where you can refresh yourself again and buy some postcards and souvenirs. Wycoller has other relics to show you. The stone vaccary walls, up to the north of where you stand towards the main road, were built to contain cattle for breeding and are probably 600 years old; if not, there were some here then.

In the election of 1959, an inhabitant of Wycoller stood for parliament as a candidate for the Lancastrian Party. The local guidebook comments: 'He returned to his home a disappointed man.' A pity.

From the craft centre follow the road over a bridge and then turn off sharp right onto a track, passing some houses on the left, over another bridge and across a stile *(3 minutes)*. In *5 minutes* cross a small stream and turn left before a stone stile and through a gap in a wall. Cross a meadow. The path is indistinct some of the way but you can see the road ahead of you, keeping the river quite close on the left. In *20 minutes* join a road and walk up to a bus stop at Laneshawbridge. Here you can get a bus to Keighley and then go by bus or train back to Haworth to finish a long day.

The walking time was nearly four hours, but you must allow six. The bus runs every hour, so check the times beforehand.

The carbound route

This is the most scenic of all the routes. The distance is a little under 30 miles but allow at least two hours to include stopping and staring. The road between Trawden and Hebden Bridge is rough, narrow and steep; so do not expect to hurry, and do be sure that the car is in good condition. This is a good route for pub lunches and for shopping, especially for Christmas presents.

You are going east from Haworth, so whichever car park you are in, you are likely to turn left and follow the signpost for Stanbury *(1.3 miles)*. If you want lunch here, I can recommend the Wuthering Heights. It is a free house with excellent food at mid-day. You pass another recommended pub called the Herders' Arms; and towards Hebden Bridge is the Packhorse Inn.

After Stanbury follow the road to Ponden *(1 mile, see the walking route)*. Here you can shop at Ponden Mill, but you can do better, though not more cheaply; there are two speciality shops between here and Laneshawbridge. The first is Scar Top Antiques which specializes, as it says, in 'stripped pine and quality reproductions.' The products do not come cheap, but to walk around is an education in itself – much more entertaining than many a so-called Folk Museum – with out-of-the way decorations and two floors full of furniture that include four-poster beds. The building is put together with pale yellow stones in numerous shapes and sizes. At a distance it looks like something out of Switzerland, near to it is even more exotic.

Back in the car, *2 miles* brings you to the county boundary, the watershed, a reservoir called Watersheddles and a chance to meet the hikers. They will have emerged from a lush valley, whereas you will have had more of the moorland scenery. To your right are Wolf Stones, to your left Grey Stones; the sinister sounds of these Pennine names tell you not to treat them lightly, while the subtle blends of browns and greens, offset by the black rocks, encourage you to stop and stare.

Another *1.5 miles* brings you to the Herders' Arms. Do stop and have lunch here if it is the right time of day. From the back of the pub you look down the steep sides of the Smithy Clough which leads to Wycoller. The hamlet is less than a mile below you, but you will have to drive round in a big circle, four miles, to get there.

After leaving the Herders you come to the other shop, Height Laithe. This is a craft shop with a difference, I would call the difference 'taste'. You are spoilt for choice among the pictures, carvings, jewellery, toys and much else; especially the carvings. You can watch the woodturning (take your own mask). There is also a non-smoking restaurant which alone is worth coming miles to discover; evening meals are by booking only.

The next village is Laneshawbridge, on the outskirts of Colne. Along this road is a view of the rounded summit of Pendle Hill in front and on the left. We are not going to Pendle Hill in this book, but take a look at the dark outline of the area famed for its witches and for its officialdom who persecuted them. Before the centre of Laneshawbridge, turn left (signpost Wycoller, *2.3 miles* from the Herders.

After that left turn at Laneshawbridge, there are two more left turns before reaching Wycoller in a little under *2 miles*. The car park is on the right just before the hamlet; from there it is only a short and easy walk, but if you are disabled you may be able to drive in. For a description, see the walking route.

On leaving the car park, follow the road out the way you came, taking the first turning left to Trawden. If you want a view of the Forest of Trawden, now bare moorland and much of it closed to visitors, you drive straight through the village and up to Hollin Hall Mill (built over a stream), *2 miles* from Wycoller. You will see that Trawden is an example of a small mill town which followed the water power to nestle under the moors. Returning to the centre of the village, turn left round the church (follow Hebden Bridge on the signpost). After *1.25 miles,* you come to Clarion House where you turn left. From here you have about *10 miles* of the most scenic, but also hairy, stretches of road in these parts. Be sure that your car and the weather are fit. There are several stretches of one in four, down and up, some sharp bends and some narrow precipitous stretches.

The road passes between the two Coldwell reservoirs which are followed by Shuttleworth Pasture. You then descend steeply into a wooded valley and out on the moors again on the other side. On the left, but out of sight of the road, is a ruin called Robin Hood's House – a reminder that the legendary outlaw was known in these parts as well as in Nottinghamshire. On the last route, you passed a pub named after Robin Hood.

The road climbs steeply and then descends past the huge Widdop Reservoir, built by the navvies who lived at Heptonstall; after this the going becomes easier and the road descends below a thousand feet for the first time for a couple of miles when you cross a stream called Greave Clough above which stand some rocks called Pisser Rough; after crossing you also cross the Pennine Way and drive down to another bridge, over a stream called Graining Water. Here you are near the Hardcastle Crags and soon reach the National Trust car park visited on the last route, following the road down through Slack to the turning circle at Hebden Bridge (just over *11 miles* from Trawden). From Hebden Bridge to Haworth, follow the route described already, a little over *eight and a half miles* back to Haworth.

Link to next route

By public transport: bus to Keighley, and bus or train to Ilkley (changing at Shipley or Leeds).

By car: from the car park exit at Haworth, right and left across the road (signpost Oakworth) down a steep hill and up the other side. Through Oakworth and Keighley (follow Skipton signs). Turn left onto the A650 at roundabout (a little under five miles). Follow the A650 to Steeton (2 miles). Then right through Silsden (A6034), turning right just after the village and across country to the A65 into Ilkley (about seven and a half miles).

On foot: There is a footpath down the valley which joins the Keighley Road beyond Oakworth. Walk through Keighley, cross the main road and the canal and walk up through Riddlesden and over the Moor into Ilkley (allow 6 to 8 hours).

Booklets

Writings on the Brontës are measured by the ton; if you want a brief and interesting account, buy the guide to the Brontë Parsonage, published by the Brontë Society.

Do read the Brontë novels, especially *Shirley* which describes the Luddite riots.

On Haworth itself there is the well-illustrated: *Haworth in Times Past* by Shirley Davids and Geoff Moore, published by Countryside Publications.

For Wycoller, see *Wycoller Country Park* by Stanley Cookson and Herbert Hindle, published by Herbert Hindle.

The Keighley and Worth Valley Railway produces a magazine called *Push and Pull*.

Charlotte Brontë did not appreciate Haworth as much as you and I. She wrote: "I can hardly tell you how time gets on in Haworth. There is no event whatever to mark its progress."

Route 7:

Ilkley Moor

The maps for this route are Ordnance Survey 1:50,000, sheet 104, and Pathfinder Series 1:25,000, sheet SE 04/14. Ilkley misses out on the Outdoor Leisure Series 1:25,000, counting in Ordnance Survey eyes as neither South Pennines nor Yorkshire Dales. The grid reference for Ilkley Town Hall is 118476. There is an information centre in the public library building opposite the station, phone no. 0943 602310. There is also an excellent local history section in the library.

Most British readers of this book will have sung about 'Ilkla Moor,' and may well have argued about what the words mean. My favourite explanation is that it was an old drinking song ('drunk as ducks') which was rewritten by a puritanical parson who was not even a Yorkshireman.

For foreign visitors there are connections with Germany, Italy, Scandinavia and the United States.

The famous Moor has much more to offer than the song suggests and so does the town itself. Let's take a quick look round the town first. Cross the road from the station or car park and visit the information centre. Outside the library building you will see a bust of Robert Collyer. You may never have heard of this character whose life was a weird example of a rags to riches story. He started life as a factory boy. At the age of eight he was working in a mill from 6 a.m. to 8 p.m., Mondays to Fridays; Saturday was a half day, work finished at 6 p.m. You had an hour for lunch and that was all. An overseer whipped you if you were caught sitting down during working hours. Collyer was one of the children who sweated to make England rich. Unlike most of his fellow workers, who died before their twenty first birthday, Robert lived to be 89, and his riches came not from commerce but from religion. He emigrated to the States and became a famous preacher. On one return visit to his native parts, he opened the building you are now looking at, hence the bust; on an earlier visit he drummed up interest in White Wells which we shall be visiting on both the walking routes. As a final gesture in old age he persuaded Leeds City Council to give him the factory bell which had summoned him to work as a child; he then presented it to Cornell University in the State of New York.

Leave the library, cross the road again, and walk down Brook Street, on the left of the station, to the river Wharfe. If you visit the river at different times of year you will hardly recognize the same Wharfe. I have seen it looking like a mountain stream, clear and sparkling; I have also watched a deep muddy torrent, high up the banks, covering the little hireboats and suggesting Niagara just round the corner. Wander along the river and back again. Then retrace your steps to the roundabout and turn right into Church Street. Inside the church is a group of Saxon crosses. Intricately carved well over a thousand years ago, these memorials of a robust christianity have entwined beasts, phallic symbols and Saint Luke with the head of a bull. Inside the church there are also memorials of an even more robust religion. Two Roman altars with arrangements for the blood to run after sacrifices and a carving of – the guidebook says – "a female figure which has given rise to many conjectures." Quite a place, Ilkley Church, and don't forget to put a fiver in the collecting box; it's cheap at the price, and someone has to clean up after you have taken your boots elsewhere.

The Saxon Crosses and Ilkley Church (the crosses are now inside the Church).

Around this area was a Roman fort built on a crossroads. One of the roads was the same as the one we encountered near Littleborough on route 3. There are reminders of this in the church, across the road on the outside of a pub and, above all, in the Manor House Museum. Here the long story of Ilkley and the Moor is told; do wander round before you go further. You will be enthralled by the pieces of evidence painstakingly put together about life in this town long, long ago; and the Moor will mean more for the experience.

How to get there

By train: from Leeds, Ilkley is the terminus of a branch line with hourly trains. There are also trains from Bradford.

By bus: frequent buses from Skipton and Leeds.

By road: Ilkley stands on the A65, Leeds to Skipton and Kendal road. This can be reached from the south by leaving the M1 at the end (exit 47) or from the north by leaving the M6 at exit 36. From Manchester and the south west follow the M66, on to the A56, then the M65, and then the A56 again through Colne turning right onto the A6068 (Keighley signpost) and left onto the A6034 (Silsden signpost) which joins the A65 near Ilkley.

Sports, hobbies and festivals

You can do most of the things that can be done in the earlier routes. You can also hire a rowing boat on the Wharfe, or go swimming in an open-air or a covered pool. The Moor has much to offer archaeologists; some of the rocks are good for climbing too, especially for learners. There is a bridge club, a dance hall and two discos in the town. There are concerts in St. Margaret's Church. There is also an amateur theatre – the Ilkley Playhouse. A special feature of the Moor is the large number of stones with prehistoric inscriptions. Some of them are over 4,000 years old; there has been much activity hereabouts for a long time.

A cup and ring stone on Ilkley Moor.

The town has its own orchestra, the Ilkley Sinfonietta, and the Wharfedale Music Festival is held in the Winter Gardens in early May.

The Ilkley Literature Festival, one of few such festivals held in the north of England (Lancaster is another), takes place every other summer; the next one is in 1988. Many famous authors have taken part in this international festival over the years including W.H. Auden, Angus Wilson and Ted Hughes. The 1986 festival had an emphasis on Indian writing and the novelist Mulk Raj Anand was among the well-known figures who came from that country.

Food, accommodation and shopping

Ilkley has less pubs and more restaurants for its size than the other towns in this book. One of the pubs, The Mallard, dates from 1709 and has been restored inside without the clutter usually considered inseparable from the historic pub.

None of the pubs I sampled for lunch appealed to me, so I suggest that the adults go to the Palm Court in the Victorian Arcade (no place for children) while junior goes to the Green Frog at the station (no place for adults). How they meet up afterwards, I will leave to their ingenuity; but the adults should take a look at both buildings. The Victorian Arcade is like a miniature of Dartmoor turned into a greenhouse. You may not have cared for Dartmoor, but it does compel a second look.

Also in the Arcade is a classy antique shop. I actually saw the staff polishing the exhibits. Not that it made much difference, they were spotless already; but the gesture was typical of the local shops. The reverse of Haworth, Ilkley goes in for international chic, not homely, home-made muddle. All is antiseptic here. You cannot help finding the right dress for the hunt ball, and for other occasions too. They take a lot of trouble these Ilkley shops, and there's a fair acreage (note the Yorkshire expression) of them. For hiking gear, you had better go back to Hebden Bridge though. Even the takeaways are called Pizza Palazzos in Ilkley. They tell me the double yellow lines used to be mauve here. Such sensible individualism must have given the Department of Transport kittens.

The afternoon tea addict has to go to Betty's, the ultimate in elegant sipping. You can get your fix of Yunnan Flowery Orange Pekoe or Cuban Extra Turquino Lavado while gaping at a huge marquetry pastoral scene. The cafe has a no smoking area, too.

In the evenings you are spoilt for choice but not for bargains. The world famous Box Tree Restaurant, I have not tried. I was told it would cost three years' profits on this book to have dinner there. That must have been a malicious exaggeration, but I can only tell you that it looks good from the outside. There are three French restaurants, a Greek, a Chinese and an Indian as well as several hotels. All those I tried were expensive but good. I particularly liked Rombald's, an elegant hotel on the way up to the Moor with impeccable service; and the Olive Tree where they go in for quantity, but the quality was OK too.

The information centre provides a long list of places to stay and is much more informative than most of those mentioned in this book. You will not expect me to have tried them all, but I did stay at some and I can truthfully recommend Mrs. Brame's, where you can have a bedroom, bathroom and sitting-room to yourself. If you are a Roman Catholic, there is a different kind of accommodation available – a retreat house.

Walking route A: The wells and the stones

Remember to look for the deliberate mistake, see the quiz at the end of the book.

I am offering two walks on Ilkley Moor. The first takes you round the sights and sites near to the town. You go over much of the Moor by a roundabout route that takes in both views and interest. The Moor is littered with paths; don't worry, the landmarks are clear. The times I've given add up to 141 minutes but allow four hours because there is a lot of stopping and staring to be done around here. You are skirting the town all the way, so it is easy to turn back if you want to. The walk is suitable for dogs Some of it would be heavy going for a pushchair; but you can see many of the sights by pushing up the first section (to just below the Cow and Calf rocks) and turning right along one of the easier paths which keeps to the base of the Moor.

A chart of both the walking routes can be found at the end of the carbound route.

Turn left from the station, past the municipal buildings on the right, and fork right up Cowpasture Road. After about *15 minutes*, when the road swings left and the end of the speed limit sign comes into view, find a small gate on the right and join a path that crosses the bridge and runs parallel to the road. When the path turns towards the south (right) follow it up among the heather and the white bilberries towards the Cow and Calf rocks which are standing up in front of you. When just below the rocks, cross another path and go straight up a slippery slope to the Calf *(15 minutes)*. After passing him on your left, scramble up the rocks on your right to the top of the Cow. If the rocks are too slippery, follow the path and approach the Cow from behind, as it were. You will be there just as soon *(5 minutes)*.

The Cow and Calf Rocks.

Award yourself a rest on top and look round. To the north you look across the town to the beginnings of the Yorkshire Dales. Nearby to the west you can see the Ilkley Crags.

I may as well tell you now that officialdom in Ilkley used to have the right ideas. A hundred years ago there was a by-law against disfiguring the rocks, removing turf, shooting and almost anything else you can think of on the Moor. That by-law seems to have been overlooked lately.

The Moor is called 'Rombalds Moor' after the giant who arranged, or rather disarranged, the rocks with which it is littered. Apparently he had a quarrel with his wife and they flung the rocks at one another. That must have been long ago-many of them bear prehistoric inscriptions. Nowadays the rocks you are standing on are used to teach climbing; they may well be crawling with little green men wearing orange helmets and with ropes strung over their shoulders. Don't worry, they are more likely to come from a local college than from Mars.

When you've finished day-dreaming, walk west towards the crags. In *3 minutes* you reach a stream; cross and turn right, following a path alongside the stream until it descends into a gorge. When the path swings left away from the stream, keep right *(5 minutes – do not turn left)* through bracken *(2 minutes)*. You then turn left and take the path which goes past the end of a row of trees and see a pond (known as The Tarn) in front of you. As you near this the path divides *(3 minutes)* and you fork left to go round the south side of the pond (which takes another *3 minutes)*; turn left at the other end up some stone steps.

White Wells.

Head for a white cottage, which soon appears in front of you, and is about *7 minutes* away. This is White Wells one of the relics of the days when Ilkley was a spa and people came to take the waters. Stand and admire the view and read the notice that says the Wells have been restored and opened to the public. These days they are usually closed to the public, but you may be allowed in at weekends. Inside you can see where the Victorian visitors plunged into the cold waters. They drank them too; for you there is tea and coffee and souvenirs. You can turn back from here if you want to. The road runs straight down to the station in less than *15 minutes.*

Walk west from White Wells (crossing the north-south track); turn left onto a path after a bridge at a double bend *(3 minutes)*. You are walking more or less parallel to a road that runs beneath you on your right. When you come to some water company manholes, in another *3 minutes,* keep straight on (do not turn right) and keep left at the next junction *(2 minutes)* through the bracken and under the trees to the road, another *2 minutes,* which you cross. You then walk straight along the wall on your right, past a reservoir. After *20 minutes,* you cross a footbridge beyond which you fork left and follow a grass path steeply upwards. Soon you can see a small fenced enclosure on the skyline. Make for this. You should reach it in *8 minutes.*

The Swastika Stone.

The 'Swastika Stone' stands within this enclosure, with its ancient carving which resembles a swastika, and dates from the Bronze Age (1500 years or so before Christ). Stand at this scenic spot on the edge of the moor and gaze north as the Pennines stretch out in front of you. Then look down at the ancient artwork and wonder what it stands for. The answer is a fertility symbol, it seems. There is nothing quite like it in this country, but there are examples of a similar design as far away as India as well as in between. Of the wandering artist, tribe, or religion nothing is known; you stand on the most mysterious spot in the mysterious South Pennines. Stop and wonder.

Leaving the Swastika Stone, retrace your steps to the footbridge; it's downhill so it should only take *5 minutes.* Just before the bridge turn left through a small gate and follow a path down the stream through a wood. Turn right before a shelter

(3 minutes) and continue along a path as it crosses and recrosses the stream. This is Heber's Ghyll, another place where it was once hoped that health maniacs would come to take the waters. They may well have felt like singing "From Greenlands Icy Mountains" when they bathed in this stream. The well-known hymn was written by one of the Heber family after whom the Ghyll is named.

Heber's ghyll.

Eventually you keep right through a gap in a fence and turning left *(5 minutes)* onto a rough road. After another *5 minutes* turn right by some bungalows and in *3 minutes* right again up some stone steps just before a house. When you reach the road, in another *3 breathless minutes,* turn right. After *5 minutes,* and just before some houses on the right, turn right on to the Panorama rocks. Sorry about all these right turns, I am taking you round in a big circle so that you will not miss these rocks.

Here is another mysterious place where ancient engravers worked. The rocks are good for scrambling; but watch the younger children, as there are some steep drops. Most of the artwork you can see is not ancient; the best of the rocks were moved a century ago to a safer place. To get there, you retrace your steps and keep on the road for *10 minutes,* all downhill for a change, until you come to Queens Road where you turn left and continue down until you see St. Margaret's Church on your right. The panorama rocks, with their cup and ring designs, are in a fenced enclosure on the left across the road from the Church. Unlike the swastika the cups and rings are common. There are many examples on the Moor.

Follow the road down for *3 minutes,* when any left turn will bring you to the station (on your left after turning right at the bottom) in about *5 minutes.*

Walking route B: Up and Over

This is the last walk I am taking you in this book, and one of my favourites. You have an hour of steep uphill graft at the beginning, after that it is downhill all the way. All the walks give a variety of scenery and interest, but this is the most varied from the heather carpeted moorlands to the valleys with a rich variety of trees and flowers. I make the walking time 174 minutes; from Ilkley to Shipley took me 5 hours, with much stopping and chatting, last time I did it.

Music lovers will like to know that they share this walk with Frederick Delius. In his youth, he followed much of the route I am recommending, wandering between Shipley and Ilkley, no doubt finding inspiration for the pastoral music he wrote later in his life.

From Ilkley station, turn right and then left up Wells Road which decants you onto the Moor in *8 minutes.* On the road is a gate and a cattle grid, before which you fork left through a small gate and up steps by a pond to White Wells *(10 minutes,* see route A). Carry on upwards and to the south along a broad path which turns into steps leading into and above the Ilkley Crags. *20 minutes* later you should reach a cairn where you cross another path. You are still climbing, but the slope is now more gentle until you reach the top in another *20 minutes.* On the way you see more cairns and some shooting boxes. At the top are two large cairns; there is also an upright stone.

STOP and admire the view – the Pennines and the Yorkshire Dales to the north, trees and fields to the east with just a glimpse of the Leeds/Bradford airport trying to spoil the scene. In front of you are acres of heather; so come in summer or autumn if possible, but the blacks and dark greens are fine at other times of year and even if the weather is bad. Among the birds are larks, meadow pippits and grouse. Among the humans, I once met a lady up here carrying a baby on her back and a heavy shopping basket in her hand. The baby-carrier was modern, but otherwise she might have stepped out of the eighteenth century especially as the man beside her was carrying nothing.

Soon you will pass a three thousand year old stone circle – known locally as the twelve apostles – and, *10 minutes* from the top, cross a little drain where you can see another standing stone on your right.

In *3 minutes* cross a wall by a stile and carry on down a steady slope, with a brief uphill at the bottom, to the next wall *(25 minutes)*. There is a farm on the left and a reservoir on the right, both at a distance from the path. Pass through this wall by an iron gate and in *7 minutes* you will reach a road, with a pub called 'Dick Hudson's' on the other side. This pub has a garden and a room for children.

When you leave Dick Hudson's go down a road signposted Eldwick and Bingley (see chart) and in *7 minutes* turn left at footpath sign.

Here the going becomes complicated, so listen carefully. The footpath brings you immediately to a farm; keep to the left, crossing two fences and a wall leaving the farm on your right and follow a fence to another wall which you cross by a stile onto a farm track *(10 minutes)*; turn right.

In *1 minute* the track turns left to some bungalows but the path goes straight on and beside a wall for *another minute*. At the next gate fork left across a field to a stile at a third gate (yet *another minute*) where the path follows a wall and soon swings right towards some buildings which have been visible in the valley since you left the track. You cross another stile before you reach these buildings in *5 minutes*. Go round them, along a track through a gate and over a stile onto a road (signpost on right reads Eldwick). This takes another *5 minutes*.

Cross the road following a footpath sign which reads: 'to the glen'. The path follows a stream under some trees, going straight over a hillock when the stream meanders to the right; stride on, beside the road, until you reach Bracken Hall Countryside Centre on your left *(20 minutes)*. Have a look inside, it has several exhibits especially designed for children but of interest to all, and buy some postcards to send to your worried relations. Then wander on, the going is easy for the rest of the way.

In *3 minutes* you will reach Old Glen House where there is a cafe and a pub; either is suitable for a snack at mid-day. The pub is a recent addition and is in a timbered building with good facilities for children.

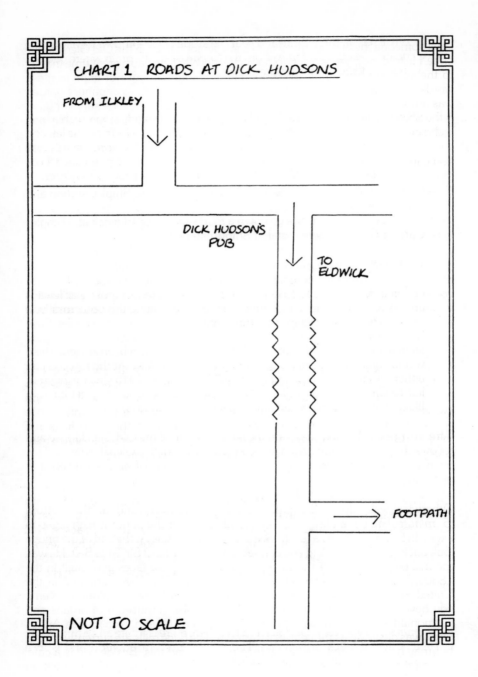

CHART 1 ROADS AT DICK HUDSONS

FROM ILKLEY

DICK HUDSON'S PUB

TO ELDWICK

FOOTPATH

NOT TO SCALE

I met someone the bureaucrats would call a senior citizen in the Old Glen House once. He told me how, as a schoolboy in World War I, he had a great time thanks to the soldiers camped on the Moor. He also told me, but not quite in these words, how the motor car had wrecked the local facilities; a Japanese garden was among the many entertainments that had disappeared. One survivor (just) is the Shipley Glen Tramway which we are going to visit. But first let me offer you a choice.

You can:

- Carry on the way I am recommending (half an hour to Shipley station and then a train back to Ilkley).

- Catch a bus from here towards Shipley station.

- Walk back the way you came (allow at least *three hours*).

- Go past the right hand side of the Old Glen House (signpost 'Bridleway') and walk down to the canal, turn right and walk along the canal until you come to two sets of locks, first three, then five in a row. The Bingley Five-Rise is one of the wonders of the canal system and still in use. This great staircase of locks strides up the hill in front of you; had it been ancient, there would surely have been a legendary giant in the offing. At the top you can either turn right to a hotel (the Hall Bank, best to book) to stay the night or left to Crossflats station for a train to Shipley if you want to get back to Ilkley (but don't leave it too late, especially on Sundays).

The suggested route starts on the left hand side of the Old Glen House and follows the road for *2 minutes* when you reach the Shipley Glen Tramway. This open air rope-hauled tramway is a must for children of all ages *when* it is operating.

Otherwise walk down the path beside the tramway and at the bottom *(5 minutes)* go left and right, cross a road and enter the park through a gap in a wall. In *2 minutes* cross a footbridge over the River Aire. At the end of the bridge look back over the park and you can see a bronze statue of Sir Titus Salt. He was the mill-owner who built the town of Saltaire that now faces you. Built in the 1850s, Saltaire was a pioneer of town planning; it has been imitated in the United States and several parts of Europe and is well worth exploring – even if you have to come back another day. There is also a museum of organs and harmoniums here. A chapel which looks like a city church from Queen Anne's reign, was designed as the centre of the town. The huge mills are currently empty, but may have been reoccupied by the time you read this. Beside you is a cafe, recommended for lunch (it opens evenings as well) and you can hire a boat on the river or (at some times of year) travel on a waterbus on the Leeds and Liverpool canal which runs just beyond. Salt allowed no pubs in his model village.

As you might expect this little gem of a northern township is under threat from the Department of Transport in London who have been playing cat and mouse with the inhabitants for as long as they can remember, threatening to build a viaduct slicing through the most beautiful part. So hurry and visit the place before it is destroyed.

Come back later if you have no time today, meanwhile turn left along the canal towpath; in *10 minutes* turn off, at the second bridge. Cross the canal and keep straight on over traffic lights to find the station on your left which you should reach in *5 minutes*.

Shipley has one of the few surviving triangular stations. The base of the triangle is for trains between Leeds and Skipton (where the line continues over the famous Settle and Carlisle railway, which is itself under threat but could be restored for the cost of a mere five miles of motorway). One side is for trains from Bradford to Skipton and the other for trains to Ilkley. They run hourly, two hourly on Sundays (but only in summer), and you may have to change at Guiseley. You pay on the train *(when* the guard bothers) and find yourself back in Ilkley in about half an hour.

Route for the carbound

There is no way you can follow the walkers over the Moor, although you can see some of the sights like the Cow and Calf Rocks, White Wells and the Panorama Stone; all you need for that is a street plan from the information centre. You can also drive down to the river and along Church Street to see the historic buildings.

The route I am suggesting gives you some treats for which the walkers may not have time, although they can easily be reached by public transport. Some of the route is on busy main roads, but I have taken you off them when possible.

From the car park by Ilkley station drive west, past the station, and straight on at the roundabout. Follow this road for *half a mile* until it joins the A65. After *one and a half miles* turn left. The signpost says 'Addingham Moorside', but you will not actually be going there; keep straight on at all junctions for a winding and hilly *three and a half miles* to join the A6034 on the outskirts of Silsden. On the other side of the town, you cross the Leeds and Liverpool Canal. There are colourful boats hereabouts called Leeds and Liverpool shortboats because the locks between Wigan and Leeds are shorter than the standard length of seventy two feet. Soon you cross the River Aire and enter Steeton over a level crossing. At a little under *two miles* since you joined the A6034, turn left at traffic lights onto the A629 for Keighley. Just under *two miles* later you come to a roundabout where you go straight on, along the A650.

As an alternative you can turn right at this roundabout; almost immediately on your right is Cliffe Castle, not a castle by 1066 standards it must be admitted, but (like the Piece Hall at Halifax) one of Britain's great unknown assets. Just to view the geology section in the Castle Museum is an eye opener if, like me, you never did know the difference between a jurassic and a silurian. Among much else, the museum has the fossilized remains of one of the earliest creatures to walk on dry land. Called a labyrinthodont it was found in a local coalmine. There are toilets for the disabled in the building as well.

Outside the castle is a cactus house where the plants grow to over six feet – I jumped up to measure them to the consternation of the local gardeners. Beyond that is a refreshment room you will be glad of, but may have difficulty getting in. It appears to be a home from school for the junior intellectuals of the town.

There is a Keighley Show early in September, if you happen to be around then. Otherwise return to the A650 and on to the next roundabout, *half a mile*. About *three quarters of a mile* later, East Riddlesden Hall is on your right. This National Trust property is a Jacobean manor house containing some elaborately carved furniture. There is a medieval barn in the grounds. *Two and a half miles* further on is Bingley Church and a turning to the left (before you get to the church) takes you to the Five-Rise locks. See the walking route B, which also tells you something about Saltaire, reached *three miles later* and just after a left fork (onto the A6038, signpost to Saltaire). Do stop, have a look round and visit the riverside cafe.

On leaving Saltaire, return to the A6038 following it to the left at Shipley (signpost Otley) Pass a mohair factory and shop. In a short distance, turn left for Baildon, *3 miles* from Saltaire). The middle of Baildon was badly knocked about in the 50s and 60s like so many other places, but it is still worth a look. Take two looks at the colourful drinking fountain in the centre, the potted meat tower the locals call it because of its pink granite. This was restored in the month I finished this book (October 1986), so we have a lot in common. Near the fountain are the stocks, no longer used, they tell me, and the remains of the market cross. There is also a large craft centre in an old mill; glass work is among the activities.

From Baildon you go over a stretch of moorland, then up and down on a narrow winding road for *6 miles* until you reach the Cow and Calf Rocks outside Ilkley. Stop and have a look before driving down the *last mile* to Ilkley station.

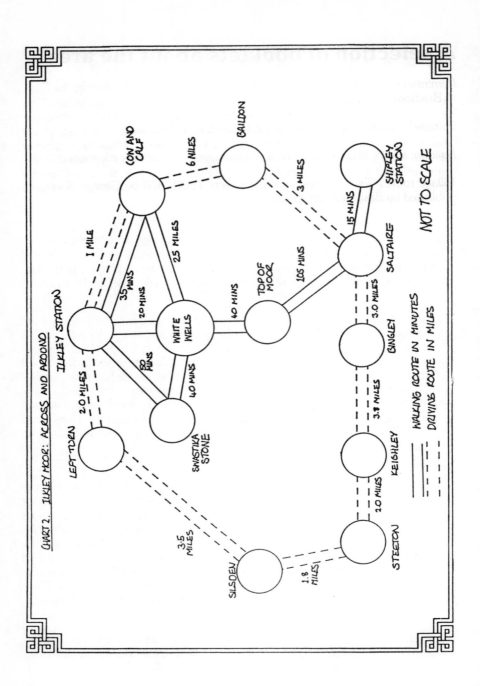

CHART 2. ILKLEY MOOR: ACROSS AND AROUND

ILKLEY STATION

COW AND CALF
BAILDON
SHIPLEY STATION
SALTAIRE
TOP OF MOOR
WHITE WELLS
BINGLEY
SWASTIKA STONE
KEIGHLEY
LEFT TOWN
STEETON
SILSDEN

6 MILES
3 MILES
15 MINS
1 MILE
25 MILES
105 MINS
35 MINS
20 MINS
40 MINS
3.0 MILES
50 MINS
40 MINS
3.8 MILES
2.0 MILES
2.0 MILES
3.5 MILES
1.8 MILES

WALKING ROUTE IN MINUTES
DRIVING ROUTE IN MILES

NOT TO SCALE

148

A selection of booklets about the area

Reminiscences of a Bradford Mill Girl by Maggie Newberry, published by the City of Bradford.

Saltaire by Jack Reynolds, published by the City of Bradford.

Baildon: a look at the past by Dorothy Burrows, no publisher mentioned.

Village to Mill Town, Shipley and its Society 1600-1870 by George Sheeran, published by Bradford Libraries.

A South Pennine Quiz

Here is a quiz to entertain you. A copy of one of the illustrations in this book, personally signed by the artist, is offered as a prize for every correct answer received.

All you have to do is to write the answers on a sheet of paper beside the numbers of the questions; there is no need to copy the questions, but be sure to get the numbers right. Send your answers to the author at 21 Barnfield, Urmston, Manchester M31 1EW. Allow at least four weeks for a reply.

(1) What is a: (a) clough?
　　　　　　(b) grough?
　　　　　　(c) booth?
　　　　　　(d) dale?

(2) What does a hill farmer mean when he describes his sheep or cattle as store?

(3) There is a private standard gauge railway in the area
　　　　(a) What is its correct name?
　　　　(b) How long is it?
　　　　(c) It has been used as a film set more than once, name one of the films.

(4) There are three canals in the area
　　　　(a) Name them.
　　　　(b) Give the length and number of locks of one of them.

(5) Name one bird that is special to the moors.

(6) List two buildings named after Robin Hood in the area.

(7) Where would you expect to find:
　　　　(a) Light Hazzles?
　　　　(b) Pisser Rough?
　　　　(c) The Cow and Calf?
　　　　(d) Ringing Roger?

(8) What is the connection between Top-o-th-Knotts, Three Lovers and Woos Nab?

(9) List the deliberate mistake on each of the walking routes.

Do not forget to add your name and address (block capitals, please) and say which picture you would like if awarded a prize.

INDEX OF TOPICS

INDEX OF NAMES